NAOMI'S HOUSES

NAOMI'S HOUSES

A Memoir

ROSALIE I. TENNISON

Copyright © 2025 Rosalie I. Tennison

All rights reserved. No part of this publication may be reproduced, stored in a retrieval system, or transmitted in any form or by any means—electronic, mechanical, audio recording, or otherwise—without the written permission of the publisher or a licence from Access Copyright, Toronto, Canada.

Heritage House Publishing Company Ltd.
heritagehouse.ca

*Cataloguing information available
from Library and Archives Canada*
978-1-77203-535-3 (paperback)
978-1-77203-536-0 (e-book)

Copyedited by Kate Kennedy
Proofread by Nandini Thaker
Cover and interior book design by Setareh Ashrafologhalai
All interior photographs are from the author's collection, unless otherwise credited.

The events detailed within this book occured on Treaty 4 Territory, which is the traditional land of the Ininew (Cree) and Saulteaux Peoples. The author is based in Winnipeg, which is located in Treaty 1 Territory, the home and traditional lands of the Anishinaabe (Ojibwe), Ininew, and Dakota Peoples. The Swan River Valley and Winnipeg are both located within the National Homeland of the Red River Métis. Winnipeg's drinking water comes from Shoal Lake 40 First Nation, in Treaty 3 Territory.

The interior of this book was produced on 100% post-consumer recycled paper, processed chlorine free, and printed with vegetable-based inks.

Heritage House gratefully acknowledges that the land on which we live and work is within the traditional territories of the lək̓ʷəŋən (Esquimalt and Songhees), Malahat, Pacheedaht, Scia'new, T'Sou-ke, and WSÁNEĆ (Pauquachin, Tsartlip, Tsawout, Tseycum) Peoples.

We acknowledge the financial support of the Government of Canada through the Canada Book Fund (CBF) and the Canada Council for the Arts, and the Province of British Columbia through the British Columbia Arts Council and the Book Publishing Tax Credit.

29 28 27 26 25   1 2 3 4 5

Printed in Canada

*In memory of my parents,
Naomi Catherine (Bradley) Tennison
and Daniel Othniel Tennison*

Naomi and Dan Tennison on their wedding day in 1947.

PROLOGUE

We went to U's sale. Saw an armchair with lids on the arms—a place for knitting and sewing. Would like to have had it but it was too big for our home.

LIFE IS all about choices. Forced to choose between two poor options, Daddy frequently had to pick the alternative that required the least amount of capital. A farmer who watched agricultural innovation change the industry over the years, Daddy's economic situation kept him in the era of the horse. When his neighbours purchased tractors and matching ploughs, he could only manage the money for a small second-hand tractor. Then he rigged his horse-drawn plough so he could control its function from the tractor via a tripwire and a length of rope to lower the blades into the ground.

At his side, Mum stoically managed the house and garden and helped him in the field or in the barn because there was no money to hire farm help. She carefully handwashed his one good shirt and ironed it to keep it ready for him to wear to church or a funeral. She mended his socks, while he repaired his overalls himself using glue and fabric salvaged from pants that couldn't take another patch.

Mum said they were a team in all things. They raised their children with firm, but loving, hands. They never contradicted an instruction or rule set by the other. Disagreements were kept away from our ears, discussed in private.

I wish I could ask them how they did it. How did they struggle on, year after year, on a money-losing farm? Were their minds and spirits bowed under by the weight of debt? When they managed to finish a room in the house or find where the water had seeped in and patch the hole, did they wish they could do better? Did they close their minds to the future in case it looked too bleak to contemplate?

I imagine them in our farmhouse during an evening in late November. The sun set several hours ago, the chores are done, and their children are sleeping under quilts and blankets in rooms where the heat from the wood stove doesn't quite reach. The frost on the thin window glass dulls the darkness that surrounds the house. In the glow of the weak overhead light and the firelight glinting through the cracks in the stove, Daddy is sitting on a wooden kitchen chair and Mum is placidly rocking. He is reading the paper to get the latest news on the price of grain, which he hopes will be better this year because his wheat crop was good. She is flipping idly through a mail-order catalogue, hoping the egg money will allow her to buy enough flannelette to make the children new pajamas for Christmas.

"I'll go to town tomorrow," Daddy says. "The cream cheque should be in."

"Can you pick up some raisins?" Mum asks. "If there is money," she adds.

He knows she would like to do some baking for Christmas. They don't have a freezer, but the coming December weather will keep her baking frozen solid in the unheated porch until it is needed.

"Do you think we can send an order next week?" She is looking at a picture of fabric with cowboys on it. Edward would love that. Lynette and Rosalie could have matching flower-patterned sets.

"We'll see. Pete said he'd pay me for the sow the beginning of the month."

The next day, Daddy arrives home from town with raisins, a pound of bologna, and a chocolate bar the family can share, but no cigarettes. He started smoking in the army, but he always places his family's needs before his habit. He knows the children are already anticipating Christmas. They start talking about Santa Claus as soon as the snow flies. He's also been trying to put aside a dime or two here and there because he'd like to get Mum some Yardley lavender soap for Christmas, the kind he sent her from overseas during the war.

"Was the cheque there?" She is happy to see the raisins, but feels badly that he didn't get a pack of Players.

"Yes, but I put most of it on the debt at the bank. We're running behind."

She watches him run his hand through his wonderful dark, wavy hair that is starting to dull with encroaching grey. She cuts his hair and he cuts the children's. She hasn't taken the time to get a haircut in several months.

"Well, I better get to the chores," he says, heading to the bedroom to change from his one good outfit into his barn clothes.

When he comes back into the kitchen, she gives him a hug and a peck on the cheek. She doesn't know what else to do when she sees the creases of worry on his forehead.

I am not a witness to their relationship. I may have been sitting on the floor playing with my doll when he got home and he would have scooped me up in his arms in a big hug after giving Mum the small sack of groceries. He might have taken me with him and let me choose the chocolate bar. While my older siblings were at school, I may have heard many exchanges between my parents, but I don't remember any. I would prefer to imagine them as happy, teasing each other and us, laughing over a story one of their children thought important enough to tell.

Our family shelter, the farmhouse, surrounded us in joy and sadness. Never quite finished, but shelter nonetheless. It had a front door no one used, because Daddy hadn't found the time or the lumber to build a step to it. Instead, we used the other door that came through the rickety porch where Tippy, our dog, lay keeping watch. The ramshackle building would never be my mother's dream home, but she did the best she could to prevent us getting slivers from the bare wood floor by covering it with hand woven rugs and cracked linoleum. She kept the wood stove stoked in the hottest summer days so we would have freshly baked bread and a surprising variety of cookies to take to school in our lunch kits.

We eventually left the farmhouse and clustered in the house that I came to refer to as "The Hovel," while a figurative wolf prowled around the exterior. Still not a dream home, we gained some modern conveniences, such as running water—even where we didn't want it.

For respite from the paucity of our homes, we escaped to Wildwood, my maternal grandparents' wonderful property, with its solidly built house that came to represent comfort and safety in our jumbled lives.

Through the challenges to keep us housed, clothed, and fed, Mum kept a diary detailing all the choices made, from forgoing the purchase of a chair that would be more comfortable than her old rocker to how much she had to shell out to dry-clean a threadbare coat. With quiet resignation, she recorded her sadness but also her joy in her children. Occasionally, she berated the houses she could never make into the one in her dream.

As I think about my parents and imagine their struggle, I am also reminded of how often they read to us. Or played a recording of a symphony on the record player Daddy bought Mum on their honeymoon. Sometimes they took us for walks through the trees on our farm and taught us to identify birdsong or to recognize the tracks of the deer, lynx, and fox that sheltered in the bushes. They excelled at "free" education that could be found in the natural world, in borrowed books, and lived experience supplied by Daddy's war years and Mum's attendance at high school in Pennsylvania.

I am assailed by a memory of Daddy reading the story about the three pigs who each live in a different house. Daddy raised pigs and, as a child, I assigned three of them parts in the tale. I assumed the pigs were our pigs. The first house is made of straw, which in hindsight fits the profile of our farmhouse. The second, made of sticks, could easily be The Hovel. Naturally, the third house would be Wildwood, with its stucco siding taking the place of brick. Of course, the moral is that the brick house saved the animals from the wolf. With the wind whistling through the poorly set windows in the farmhouse, I related to the pigs and I hoped that someday I would live in a sturdier house.

Despite the hard choices and the struggle, Mum and Daddy, like most parents, wanted their children to have a better life. I wish I could tell them I appreciate their hard work and assure them that we did okay.

THE FARMHOUSE

Dan and Edward Tennison driving Rusty
and Jumbo, hitched to the sleigh.
The farmhouse is in the background.

When others claim Danny's time and my walls do not get sided up, I think to myself, "What does it matter with Danny, Lynette and Edward to love." Otherwise, I could not stay happy... I so very much want to get our home fixed up nicely for the children to grow up in—a room for each one, shelves for our books, new floor covering and some pretty furniture. They say one cannot live on love alone, but sometimes I think that we are doing just that!

IF LUCK IS a genetic trait, it doesn't run in my family. I learned at a young age that money is precious and is not to be spent on gambling. When I wanted a stuffed toy at the local fair, Daddy said he didn't have the money to lose on a game of chance. My parents did buy tickets on various draws, but the money was considered a donation to help the cause because their ticket was never pulled. Instead, we learned to create our own good fortune. When Mum's quilt, covered in meticulous tiny stitches, won first prize, it was the result of her hard work and not luck. I have won prizes, too, but only after I crafted a better sweater or essay than my competitors.

Meanwhile, my "donations" to raffles have netted me, at best, the last-place prize that no one wants to win.

Therefore, it must have been an unlucky wind blowing across the prairies that did an extra swirl around the quarter section of land that would become my family's home. Virgil's phrase "love conquers all" so aptly describes my parents' struggle, even as they were buffeted by economic challenges and human unkindness. Through the threat of war, family conflict, health scares, and frequently thwarted dreams, they stood fast together using their love as a shield to protect us from the poverty beating down our lives. I think they believed that as long as they had each other they could survive anything—and maybe they would have. But the ill wind blew away their dreams until all that remained were their hopes for their children.

Our farmhouse was Daddy's labour of love for Mum but, despite his desire to give her the house of her dreams, it never got finished. I know little about its origin other than what my older siblings tell me. He built the house to save her from sharing his meddling mother's dwelling. Constructed on the edge of a quarter section of Manitoba farmland, the house, despite its lack of running water and electrical power (until the 1950s), was basic, but it was theirs.

Our farm, located near the fifty-second parallel in the southwest of the province but still several hundred kilometres north of the large southern population that hugs the United States border, was originally owned by my paternal grandparents. Even in the twenty-first century it takes between three and four hours to drive to larger towns and cities to the south and west from this remote area. Roughly thirty kilometres north of our farm, vast tracts of forest, muskeg, and the Canadian Shield stretch to the shores of Hudson Bay.

Our rocky fields provided us with a regular family activity. My siblings, mother, and I picked rocks while Daddy guided the horses over the poor soil. We walked behind the stone boat, a flat platform on skids, adding to the growing mound of fieldstone on it. The rocks I chose were the smallest and may not have hindered crop production, but I couldn't be left alone in the house. Our collections were added to several rock piles around the farm that became havens for small animals.

No potable water could be found on the property. Several wells dug over the years were abandoned when the water proved to be undrinkable. Our parents, worried we might fall in, warned us to stay away from the capped wells. The newest well at the edge of the yard near the barn and chicken coop served the animals and provided water for the garden. Daddy had a dugout created to get more water for the livestock. We were forbidden to swim in the deep hole and were cautioned not to drink its water either.

My brother Edward and I played on the clay hill created by the dugout's construction. He taught me the principle of skipping stones across the water, although I never mastered the technique. We also collected gypsum crystals that were exposed during the excavation. The crystals glittered like diamonds on the hill after heavy rain. We competed to see who could find the largest.

Daddy hauled cooking and drinking water in ten-gallon milk cans from a neighbour's farm a mile away. As a child, I couldn't understand why drinkable water could be so close to us and yet our water remained off limits. If Daddy went to town to pick up our mail, buy groceries Mum needed, or get machinery parts and animal feed, he would also bring back cans of water.

As I consider my family's story, I wonder why my Tennison grandparents purchased such a poor piece of property and then insisted their son buy it from them. He agreed to the sale rather than seek a better piece of land elsewhere in the district. As it turned out, he had to borrow the money he needed to buy the land. So why didn't he spend the loan on a quarter section of better, less rocky soil with potable water? I ache for him over the guilt he likely felt while our family lived with the adverse consequences of his buckling under pressure from his mother, Agnes (Grandma Tennison to us, and never just Grandma).

The farm's initial owner built a house on the property, but we don't know what happened to it or why my grandparents did not live in it. As long as we lived there, we were warned away from a low spot where the original house had sat. It seems to me that our farm was littered with holes that could swallow small children! For some reason, my grandparents chose to build another house. Edward says they salvaged two-by-fours from a silo on the property and built what I called a log cabin because of the exposed wood. Daddy took Mum to that "cabin" after their wedding.

The two cohabiting couples set disaster in motion. Grandma Tennison developed a dislike for Mum because she took her only remaining son. She never wanted Daddy to marry and had expected him to care for her in her old age. My mother—young, pretty, and in love—likely reminded my grandmother of the youthful hopes and dreams she'd put aside for marriage.

Agnes Phelps Tennison loved her hats. In the most memorable photos we have of her she is wearing spectacular hats. She aspired to be a milliner and, after taking dressmaking classes in her hometown of Ingersoll, Ontario, she intended to begin her hat construction training. She must have needed money to pay for the millinery course or she wanted adventure, because she joined a "harvest train" heading west from Ontario. The western farmers needed workers to stook and stack the wheat sheaves, then feed them into the threshing machines' gaping maws. Trains from the east snaked across the Prairies transporting threshing crews to help get the crops binned before winter. This hard, dusty work paid well, and many harvesters used the money they earned to return to Toronto or other parts east in search of easier work, to set themselves up in a small business, or buy land. Agnes's dream of becoming a milliner got put aside when, somewhere during her western journey, she met my grandfather, George Tennison.

Grandpa Tennison grew up on a farm near Sarnia, Ontario, but, as a younger son, his hopes of taking over the farm were slim. When George and Agnes married, they acquired a farm property in Dand, Manitoba, a small community near Melita. My father, Dan, born there in 1907, jokingly told us the town had been named after him. Relatives wrote to them saying there was good land available in the Swan River Valley and the couple moved north with their son. They retained ownership of the southern land renting it out. My grandparents must have misread the part in the letter about good land because the quarter section they purchased eight kilometres east of Bowsman was anything but fertile. Why my grandparents chose that particular parcel of land is a mystery. The only explanation I have is that it may have been the one piece for sale in an area where they wanted to settle.

I think homesteading life was hard even with good land. At the beginning of the twentieth century, regular pregnancies, infant mortality, and hard work aged women prematurely. Men were often sidelined by illness or accidents. Attempting to make a go of it on their property, my grandparents were aided by Daddy as soon as he was old enough to handle a team of horses. Eventually he became one of the area's most chased bachelors, but he only had eyes for a blond, blue-eyed beauty thirteen years his junior.

In isolated rural areas miles from a town and with no theatres or other entertainments, the homesteaders created their own fun, often centred around the one-room schoolhouses that dotted the landscape. In the summer, picnics and baseball tournaments brought families together. Variety concerts and dances chased away the winter darkness. The men pushed the desks to the walls and someone with a fiddle would start playing dance tunes. If the school had a piano, a small ensemble would form to play waltzes, polkas, and, since many of the homesteaders at the time were from the United Kingdom, English country dances. Often one of the men would jump to the front of the room and call out the steps for square dances. Everyone danced. Parents taught their children the schottische and the butterfly. Many years later, worried her teenager lacked social abilities, Mum tried to teach me the steps to the Sir Roger de Coverly. She wanted me to be able to take part, if asked, at the barn dances frequently held in our area. Sadly, I never got the hang of it, probably because it is a hard dance to do with only two people!

Folks travelled from district to district for the dances and to have a chance to catch up on news with friends. The men tended to the fires and checked on horses stabled in the barns. Occasionally, one of them had been to town returning with a case of beer the others would pitch in to pay for and share. The women put out lunches of sandwiches and cake partway through the evening to give the dancers and musicians a break.

Daddy spied Mum when she was a young teen and asked her to dance. They were a classic fairytale couple. He tall, dark, and handsome and she a fair five foot, two inches. But not everyone shared my father's opinion of Mum as a picture of perfection. During one dance, my mother overheard two of her neighbours talking about them. Before Daddy swung her out of hearing range, one woman said to the other, "Naomi would have a perfect figure if she didn't have such thick ankles." Daddy didn't care; he liked the whole package and even ended an engagement to someone else so he could wait for Mum.

The budding romance had to be put on hold while Mum went to Pennsylvania for three years to attend high school. They reunited shortly after her return to Canada, but then endured another separation while Daddy went to war. They rekindled the romance as soon as he returned from overseas and he proposed. At twenty-six, she had been labelled a spinster even though the war had reduced the number of available men. When she asked him why he'd waited so long, he said, "I had to wait for you to grow up."

Within months of their marriage, they anticipated the arrival of their first child, my sister Lynette. My maternal grandmother gave her daughter eggs because the Tennison farm had no laying hens. But Grandma Tennison would not let Mum eat more than one egg, while everyone else had two or three. She said to my pregnant mother: "You're too fat."

Nothing my mother did could please her mother-in-law. They shared an interest in making quilts, but Mum's seams were crooked or her chosen pattern did not impress my grandmother. Grandma Tennison's sour disposition took its toll on my shy, sensitive, pregnant mother.

Midway through her pregnancy Mum left Daddy to return to her parents, Harley and Iva Bradley. Forced to choose between his wife and their expected child and his parents, Daddy chose Mum. He asked his parents to move to Bowsman so his wife could return to him. When his father died of a heart attack shortly after they settled in town, Daddy must have suffered great guilt. However, my sister's arrival in August would wash away some of the sorrow. Daddy's joy could not be contained when he became a father at forty.

Daddy began building a new house the year Lynette turned two. He didn't want his family living in one that still contained his mother's things. Though it was the most basic of shelters and remained largely unfinished, the structure he built became a home filled with love. My early recollections of the farmhouse are fleeting and often triggered by a sight, sound, or smell. Using my index finger, I drew hearts and stick people in the frost that formed on the single pane windows that also rattled when the wind blew. When I take bread out of my electric oven, the smell reminds me of Mum removing her loaves from the wood stove's oven. When I visit the dean's office at the College of Agriculture and Biosciences at the

University of Saskatchewan in Saskatoon for work, the canola design in the floor reminds me of the flowers on the linoleum in our farmhouse. We chose the new flooring as a family in the small Bowsman Co-op store. When we got home, Daddy unrolled the fresh sheet of linoleum and my imagination soared. It looked like a magic carpet from my storybooks, with a solid colour centre and a floral border.

I know the bones of the original house. Split in the centre by a staircase ascending to an unfinished and poorly insulated upper area, the main floor had a front half and a back half. A combination kitchen and living room contained a wood stove, piano, table, and collection of wooden chairs. Two bedrooms shared the back half of the house. You entered the first after passing round the base of the stairs and then you walked through it into the second bedroom. A door in the second bedroom, hidden by a curtain, gave entrance back into the front half of the house. None of us can remember why we never pushed aside the curtain to gain access to the room our parents slept in. A cupboard under the stairs, dubbed "the treasure trove," contained our games. Minimal storage meant items were stuffed wherever they could fit. I don't remember having closets, but we probably didn't need them because we had only a few items of clothing.

Grandpa Bradley poured a cement basement for my parents and then Daddy built the house over it. The lower space is dank and dark in my memory. Mum stored all her canned goods in that cellar. She would run down into the black hole and return with a two-quart jar of canned beef she combined with vegetables and topped with dumplings for a savoury stew. I never went down there because the darkness worried me. Merely utilitarian and not intended for living, the cellar served its purpose for food storage and supported the structure above.

The cabin that had been my grandparents' home became derelict over time but it remained on the property near our house and reminded us of them. Daddy still viewed it as his parents' home and, as far as I know, he never went inside. After my grandfather died, Grandma Tennison moved back to Ontario, where her daughter Jean had settled in the 1930s. Taking only her clothes, Grandma Tennison left trunks containing household items in her former house. As I ran around our farm, I received many cautions not to go into the cabin because it, like the sinking hole beside it marking the location of the original house, was unstable.

On the rare occasions Grandma Tennison came to visit, she spent her time in the rickety cabin sorting through her trunks. Mum said she would bring items into the house—a pressed glass dish, for example—show it off, and then return it to the trunk in the cabin. I bet it became a contentious issue between my parents that serviceable items stored metres from our house could not be put to use by our family. Daddy warned us never to touch his mother's trunks and we didn't. Those trunks continued to be our responsibility after my father's and grandmother's deaths and, in the end, we shared very little in their hidden bounty.

A few months after they moved into the new house, Mum gave birth to Edward. My parents believed their perfect family would include four children. However, despite what they might have wanted, the next pregnancy did not happen for several more years.

*Danny went to town and took chickens; got $16.50
for them. It is hard to find money for groceries
these days and I wanted a few things for Christmas.*

A JOVIAL MAN, Grandpa Tennison taught his eldest son to be hardworking and honest. Frequently, neighbours would refer to Daddy as being "just like Pa." However, a strong work ethic and sense of humour couldn't make the rocky land north of the farmhouse profitable.

The poor excuse for a farm required a great deal of hard labour to eke out any kind of living. When the Depression ravaged farms across the Prairies, my grandparents sent Daddy, barely into his twenties, south to farm their quarter section near Dand. Drought and wind destroyed everything and Daddy lined up at the train station to get vegetables sent by kind gardeners with excess produce. He once gratefully accepted two large, overly mature beets that he cooked for an hour trying to get them soft enough to eat.

Eventually, the family gave up on the Dand farm and Daddy returned to Bowsman not long before war was declared in Europe. A thirty-two-year-old volunteer when he joined up, Daddy was older than many of the fresh-faced recruits turning up to serve. He felt a duty to sign up, but I also believe that he, like many other farm boys, saw it as an adventure and a way to see the world.

For Mum, the Second World War came with constant worry about the safety of the boys she'd grown up with and who were now facing danger on the other side of the world. She and her friends corresponded faithfully with all of them, but she looked forward to Daddy's letters the most. When the dreaded posting of casualties, or telegrams telling of the missing and dead, didn't contain my father's name, she breathed easier. Before he shipped overseas, Daddy released Mum from their romance saying she didn't have to wait for him, but she did. Thankfully, he didn't bring another bride home with him because I think that would have broken her heart.

Daddy spent most of the war in Europe, where an army on the move couldn't stop at banks. The soldiers received a stipend to pay for cigarettes, beer, and gifts for sweethearts, but the bulk of their salaries were sent home to their families. Salaries for the single men were delivered to their mothers, and most banked it so their sons would have a nest egg when they came home.

My father's war experience was probably as horrendous as most. A sergeant in the medical corps, he must have seen a lot of gore and suffering. After the war, Daddy always scraped together a dollar or two for The War Amps. I think he was trying to support the amputees he may have helped off the battlefield. He never talked about the horror he saw. Instead, he chose to tell us amusing stories about how his unit celebrated Christmas or what he did when he had leave and could meet friends and relatives in Paris or London. He often told us about seeing Mount Etna erupting in Sicily. In Italy, he developed a taste for strong, black coffee that he claimed kept his hair black. He maintained a correspondence with a lady in Scotland who billeted him during his training and who, after he returned home, sent wonderful gifts. Mum said the war fostered his interest in medicine and Daddy dreamed of being a doctor. Instead he came back to the farm and a constant struggle for survival. Farm work entailed killing animals, a job he hated. He had seen enough killing.

Daddy faced an unexpected financial challenge when he returned home. My selfish grandmother had put his army pay in her bank account rather than opening one in his name like other mothers did. She never gave Daddy a penny of his service pay on his return from overseas. Without his own money, he had to borrow from the Veterans' Land Act, set up to help returning soldiers purchase farmland, stock, and equipment. His parents wanted a good price for their farm and he had to borrow the entire amount. He disliked owing money and he struggled to make the payments. We grew up with the idea, impressed upon us by him, that borrowing is always a bad idea and should never be considered a first solution to a financial problem.

When he came home from overseas, Daddy wanted to marry my mother and start a family. Returning servicemen could get financial assistance to go to university but it meant living in a city. He did not want to saddle Mum and their future children with the life of a struggling student. He hadn't completed high school because his parents told him he had to work on the farm so his younger sister Jean could get an education. Without a high school diploma, he would need to take remedial classes to get the prerequisites for medical school. He might have been fifty by the time he finally got a medical license. As I consider his decision to keep farming, I wonder if it was really a choice between two imperfect options. His cash-strapped family struggled as much on the farm as we might have in the city while waiting for him to become a doctor. On the farm, however, we grew our own food.

In a discussion with Mum's older brother, Henry, who also spent time overseas, Daddy expressed regret that he didn't stay in the army. Despite the war being over, concern there could be another had prompted the Canadian government to fund a permanent armed force for the country. The returning soldiers from "the war to end all wars" in 1919 had gone back to their previous lives. When the Second World War broke out, Canada had to rely on volunteers like my father to leave their farms and fight again. This time, returning soldiers were offered pensions if they signed up to stay in the military for seven more years. The pension would have helped him move forward in life with a regular income. Instead he moved back to the farm, married Mum, and embarked on a life of familial joy overshadowed by poverty. While he might have regretted that choice, he never regretted his family.

I left for the hospital and arrived there at 12:25 AM.
Our baby girl was born at 12:50 PM She cried
until around 7:00 o'clock from hunger they tell me.

"YOU WERE BORN on the night of the red northern lights." It's a phrase I heard throughout my childhood, and because Mum never missed an opportunity to educate, I learned early on that they were also known as the aurora borealis. I grew to love the poetic sound of those Latin words.

The auroras are frequently seen in both the northern and southern hemispheres. Where I grew up, cold, lightless winter nights were brightened by the dancing colours. I loved watching the magical movement of yellow and blue and green out the car window as we drove home from visiting neighbours or relatives. An uncommon colour for an aurora display is red; the result of oxygen molecules at higher altitudes.

The red lights circled the Canadian Arctic for over two thousand kilometres the night I entered the world, according to scientific records of the event. Perhaps that is why my favourite colour is red or why my arrival in the Birch

River Hospital happened quickly. I didn't want to miss the lights that tinted the snow pink with reflected colour and shone with a rouge glow through the hospital windows.

In those days, especially in winter, having a baby required some coordination. Our farm was twenty-two kilometres from the small hospital in Birch River. Dr. A.H. (Alfred Henry) Boon, our family doctor, would help Mum give birth to her third child—me. A larger hospital in Swan River, where my sister Lynette had been born, was thirty kilometres away and too far to travel in the winter. The small town of Bowsman, where we did our shopping and delivered eggs to the train station, didn't have a hospital. The eight-kilometre difference between Swan River and Birch River from our farm in the 1950s may as well have been fifty for a family relying on a 1930 Plymouth for transportation. Our more reliable winter transportation—a team of horses hitched to a wooden box most often used for hauling grain—wouldn't be fast enough to get a woman in labour to a hospital in frigidly cold weather or a snowstorm.

To keep Mum safe, my parents made a plan. Her February 14 due date landed on a Friday. Arrangements were made during my mother's last visit to the doctor for her to await her baby's arrival at the Birch River home of the Bishop's Messengers of St. Faith's, an evangelistic outreach organization sanctioned by the Anglican Church of Canada. On February 10, the entire family delivered Mum to her temporary home, a small white clapboard cottage.

Prone to precipitate births, Mum delivered each of her children faster than the one before. I showed up in record time somewhere between a half hour and an hour. Perhaps I could hear the talk about the red northern lights as folks arrived for an evening of cards at St. Faith's on the tenth. Mum, physically uncomfortable and already thinking her delivery time was approaching, asked the St. Faith's messenger to call a cab to take her to the hospital. She vowed to look at the auroras en route. In her great discomfort, she required help getting into the cab. Later, she remembered noticing the snow was tinted pink, but she forgot to look up.

Once Mum got into the hospital, I arrived in short order. Apparently, I wouldn't shut up while my mother caught her breath. Worn out by my rapid arrival, Mum could not breast-feed. The nurse said I wanted beefsteak but "we settled her with a bottle instead."

Meanwhile, the vivid red sky prompted Daddy to rouse my siblings from bed, taking them outside to look up at the show, not knowing the latest family member had arrived. My family didn't have a telephone, but Daddy and my siblings planned to go back to the hospital the following Sunday to learn if Mum had given birth on Valentine's Day. On his own, Daddy capably managed to get Edward and Lynette the short distance to the one-room Craigsford School with proper lunches and warm clothing. He did his best to fix Lynette's hair, cook meals, and continue his daily chores of looking after animals.

I ruined my family's careful plans by arriving three days early in the wee hours of February 11. Even though we didn't have a telephone, our community was replete with gossips, aided by a party line. Word got out fairly quickly that Mum was safely delivered of a baby girl. My siblings learned about me at school when my cousins arrived with the news. Their mother, Auntie Rene, had telephoned the hospital to check on her sister.

Lynette says she desperately wanted a little sister and frequently went outside on starry nights to wish on a star for one. I think she bought into the movie images of sisters trading outfits. With us, it would be a one-way exchange: I would get her hand-me-downs. As adults, I could never fit into her dresses or blouses. Always welcome to mine, my clothes hung on her slight frame.

Arriving home from school that day in great distress at being upstaged because she would not be the one to share the happy news that she had a sister, Lynette's tears burst forth. Daddy may have been happy to learn his wife and new daughter were healthy, but any joy was tempered by Lynette's unhappiness. Daddy couldn't understand why our family and neighbours would think it their duty to relay this important information. Surely they could have assumed my parents had their own plan in place to announce their news. It wasn't the last time the party line violated our family.

Four days after the red northern lights faded and news of my birth had spread to every corner of our district, my family arrived to meet me. Dr. Boon wrote a receipt for fifty dollars for our time in the hospital and we set off for home in the 1930 Plymouth. Finding the cash to pay my delivery bill must have been a struggle for my parents. They may have been saving since the discovery of Mum's pregnancy. If I could ask her, I know Mum would reply: "You were worth every cent."

My arrival brought great joy by most accounts. But, until dementia took over her mind, Mum couldn't forget the disappointment of those ruined plans. She repeatedly told us how my father was provoked by the neighbourhood busybodies' actions that pointed out how he couldn't afford a telephone for his family. The pre-emptive announcement of my birth, removing it from my parent's control, joined a list of seemingly minor slights that inadvertently amplified our poverty. On one later occasion, Mum was asked to order a book for someone to ensure the package didn't arrive at the home of the recipient, but was never reimbursed when it was collected. Too timid to ask more than once, she never received payment. Instead, she scrimped on groceries to cover the debt. Throughout her life, Mum paid directly and indirectly for the boorish behaviour of others, and having her oldest daughter told at school that she had a sister was a discourtesy of the highest order.

I arrived in my first house on a chilly February 16, 1958. For the first few weeks, I likely lived close to the wood stove but my parents' bedroom had a crib as well. When I learned to crawl and then walk, I spent my time on the floor playing with my treasured set of plastic farm animals while Mum cooked and baked. I used the domino set to create corrals and pens for horses, cows, pigs, and chickens. I became hysterical when my younger cousin, Twila, chewed the tail off my lovely white plastic foal. In hindsight, chewing the foal saved the other thing she liked to chew on—me! Mum would rescue me and apply cold compresses to the rather large bite marks I received from her.

My other favourite toy showed up under the Christmas tree. I marvelled that Santa Claus would give me a doll wearing pajamas that matched the set he left for me. Years later, I found the flannel scraps Mum tucked away after construction of the matching sleepwear. With a hard plastic head and a rubber body, the doll had a great deal of flexibility. One afternoon, Mum found me up to my elbows in the wash basin with my toy folded into the curve of the pan. The doll, covered with mounds of soap suds, and I, wet nearly from head to toe, must have been a shocking, yet funny, sight.

"Honey, what on earth are you doing?" Mum asked.

"I'm giving Naomi Catherine a bath," I replied, naming her on the spot.

"Well, I think she's clean enough. Perhaps we should rinse the soap out of her eyes and get her dry before she catches cold." Mum grabbed the hand towel off the nail by the basin. Years later, she told me how flattered she was that I named my doll after her.

Despite neighbours, family, and Dr. Boon believing I was an "accident," the community got another shock when Mum gave birth to my younger brother, Gareth, about three years after me.

Grandma Tennison came to visit while our family was preparing for the arrival of its newest member. The woman had terrible timing. It's not as though she was coming to help her daughter-in-law during what turned out to be a difficult pregnancy. Instead, she used our house as a stopping off point while she visited cousins and friends. Her arrival, comings and goings, and unpleasant demeanour made my mother's discomfort worse. But Mum said she tried to be as kind and polite as possible, knowing Daddy wanted his children to know their paternal grandmother. In fact, the woman terrified me. She had a huge goiter and, with her grey hair and dark clothing, became my inspiration for the witch picture I created in Grade 1 for Halloween.

During my grandmother's visit, Mum often lay down to get relief from her morning sickness. She usually took me with her but sometimes I didn't want to have a nap. To keep me occupied while she rested, Mum would suggest I shell the great northern beans my family planted every year for use in baked beans and soup throughout the winter. She set up a shelling station for me near the stove with a basket of picked beans, a bucket for the dry shells that would be burned in the stove, a bowl for the shelled beans, and a little stool. I would sit there shelling beans until boredom set in. One day, my screams woke

Mum from her fitful sleep and brought Daddy running from the barnyard. When asked what had happened, my grandmother shrugged.

"Honey, what's wrong?" My mother, unable to lift me, looked helplessly at Daddy.

"Girlie, what's wrong?" Daddy swept me into his arms.

"Is she hurt?" Mum asked.

"Miiiibeeeens, miiiibeeeens," I wailed.

When they looked at my corner where my stool and various receptacles sat, everything had been cleaned up and put away.

"Mother, did you shell Rosalie's beans?" Daddy looked at his mother for an answer.

"Those beans weren't going to shell themselves and leaving chores like that undone is an eyesore," Grandma Tennison huffed.

Daddy set his jaw. "That messy corner is Rosalie's. She likes to shell beans and we let her help. It gives her something to do. When she shells every bean in her bucket, we give her more. In future, do not touch anything in that corner."

After berating his mother, Daddy took me to the farmyard and sat me, still sniffling, on some hay so he could see me while he worked. Mum likely returned to their bedroom to lie down, but also to avoid her mother-in-law. Meanwhile, Grandma Tennison probably harrumphed around the house looking for something else to tidy to show up my mother's housekeeping. From then on, I gave Grandma Tennison a wide berth. I have no memories of ever sitting on her knee or receiving a hug from her.

I only ever saw Grandma Tennison once more in my life. I think of her differently today than how I viewed her as a terrified child. She put aside her ambition for love and family, which couldn't have been easy. Mum told me she calculated, from what her mother-in-law revealed, that Grandma Tennison had been pregnant at least thirteen times. Daddy recalled being told to be quiet because his mother was sick in bed. His father would leave the house and come back a short time later with a wooden box he had hastily hammered together in the barn. He would take the box into the bedroom and return quickly to carry it outside. Daddy never saw the boxes again. In the Bowsman cemetery, there are markers by my grandfather's grave that are just labelled "Baby." To our knowledge, only five of the pregnancies produced a child that received a name, and my uncle Ivan died in infancy. My teenage uncles, Harold and Arthur, drowned together in a river on the same day. Only Daddy and his younger sister Jean reached adulthood. With so much tragedy and hardship, it's no wonder Grandma Tennison seemed unhappy.

Meanwhile, Mum stoically suffered her mother-in-law's presence and terrible morning sickness. My rapid entry into the world had damaged Mum's uterus, so I am somewhat to blame for her discomfort. Dr. Boon, the kind country doctor who delivered me, did not advise Mum to avoid another pregnancy, believing the "accident" myth. When she arrived at his office joyously announcing another baby was on the way, Dr. Boon told her he would have strongly counselled against it had she told him a fourth child was desired.

In 1960, a new super drug touted to ease the discomfort of morning sickness hit the Canadian market. But Dr. Boon advised her to "tough it out" because he believed there hadn't been enough testing on thalidomide. He didn't want to prescribe it unless Mum felt she couldn't take any more illness. So Gareth avoided the effects of thalidomide, but other issues challenged him.

Born prematurely, in the days of small country hospitals with no neonatal intensive care unit, Gareth died before reaching his first birthday. My family held a small remembrance ceremony for my baby brother at our house and placed him in a tiny wooden coffin made by Grandpa Bradley.

"He looked so angelic, I just wanted to take him out of the little box to keep him safe," Lynette recalled when we visited the small plot in the Bowsman cemetery that swallowed his remains. Mum mourned her "sweet baby boy" for the rest of her life.

Mum said that for several days after Gareth died, before she packed away the items that had surrounded him, I busied myself in the places he had been. I tidied the changing table by straightening the diapers and I pulled the sheet over the thin mattress in his little crib. My baby brother has always been part of my life, but I don't remember his cry or the touch of his hand.

[W]e poured cement for our new kitchen.
I shovelled gravel into the mixer. In the afternoon,
Danny and I threshed. I am so tired.

DESPITE HAVING a smaller family than planned, my parents decided we were outgrowing our house. An amazing cook and baker, Mum needed a better kitchen and more space to work. She made us wonderful birthday cakes, artfully cutting slab and round cakes into abstract pieces that she arranged into new shapes. The results would be iced and decorated to become sailboats, an elephant (that was mine), rabbits, and other creatures. I still marvel at what she did with only a wooden kitchen table for kneading bread, whipping cream, mixing and decorating cakes and cookies, and preparing vegetables and meat for canning. The bowls, spoons, pans, jars, and everything else to accomplish these tasks were stored on rough shelving and in boxes.

With the help of family, the existing house received an addition. Our former back door became the opening into the new kitchen. The older space evolved into a full living room. Mum's joy at having a set of cupboards to store all the items she needed to feed and celebrate her family knew no bounds.

My imaginary friends—Cicero, Mrs. Carrot, and Petunia (a lovable talking pig who walked upright on her back legs)—and I spent many hours playing on the stairs that descended through a dirt and gravel crawl space from the new section into the cellar under the original house. I invented plays that I would try to perform for my family as they stood at the top of the stairs. Mum, working in the kitchen, didn't have to see me to know I was okay because I talked to my friends all the time. Mrs. Carrot, a teacher (probably inspired by Lynette, who practised her instruction skills on me), tried to teach Cicero, Petunia, and myself whatever a five-year-old mind could imagine. Daddy had a pig called Petunia and I don't know if that is where I conjured an anthropomorphic animal friend for myself or if Daddy named the pig after my friend. I have no idea where the name Cicero came from. It makes sense that it might be from something Mum read to me. The four of us spent many hours on the stairs going down to the cellar under the original part of the house.

The construction of the new section of our house fascinated me. I followed my uncles, grandfather, and father as they hauled two-by-fours and plywood to the site. Today, a small child running around a construction site would result in calls to Children's Services. Under foot most of the time, I learned not to step on the Gyproc (as drywall was commonly referred to back when there was only one manufacturer) nailed on the underside of the two-by-fours that created the lower room's ceiling. I hopped from beam to beam like the cats did in the barn.

The men ran the wiring in the house and I eagerly collected the circular bits of metal they punched out of the junction boxes and threw on the ground. I amassed a fortune in these "coins," but I also helpfully kept the job site tidier.

The pretty pink fluff put between the two-by-fours to insulate the addition reminded me of the cotton candy my parents once bought me at the local fair. Occasionally, bits of it would fall to the ground or a chunk would be cut out to make room for a junction box. I eagerly pounced on it before one of the men told me not to touch it because its itchiness would give me a rash.

I ran barefoot that summer and picked up the nails they dropped, reducing the number I or anyone else could step on. As it was, I spent many an evening soaking a foot in warm salt water after a nail punctured my skin. My baby records show I had a tetanus shot, but Mum, whose father survived tetanus, did not want to take chances with me. I sat impatiently with my foot in the pan to ensure no poison entered my bloodstream.

As part of the renovation, Lynette got her own room in the upstairs of the older house. The previously unfinished space had a dormer window and she got a closet. The move upstairs removed her from the top bunk and Edward's torments. He liked poking her in the back with his baseball bat. I suspect my parents had plans that

Lynette and I would eventually share the new room, but that never happened. I thought it a great adventure if she asked me to sleep with her. Edward was to get a room in the space over the new addition, but that never happened either. Instead, the sleeping arrangements got shuffled while we waited for the house to be finished. Too small for the top bunk, I began sleeping with Mum. Daddy, who was up early and suffered shoulder pain from pitching sheaves and carrying water and animal feed, began sleeping in the top bunk. I wonder now if my parents ever had any alone time or if they just became partners trying to make ends meet on our money-losing, heavily-in-debt farm. As I look back on how hard they tried to give us a comfortable home, I am saddened by how often their plans were thwarted and how their love must have been tested.

A small room off the new kitchen housed the cream separator that Daddy used every morning and night when he finished milking cows. The galvanized tub in which we took our weekly baths sat in this small room. These were the get in, scrub off, get out kind of baths because the water cooled off quickly and the small tub was not designed to encourage languishing. We did not have running water, but I suspect this room would have become a bathroom if that had ever been arranged for the house.

In the winter, Mum warmed my pajamas by the fire while I splashed in the tub. Once clean and dry, I put on the flannelette nightwear and snuggled into bed. Looking back, I marvel at how protected and loved we were. Mum embroidered my initials on my pajama top and added lace around the collar of Lynette's. Edward might get some dark piping on his cuffs and collar. While the neighbours might be looking at our family with sympathy because Daddy didn't have a better car or Mum wore the same coat for years, inside our house we were warm, loved, and believed we were well off because we had nicer pajamas than could be found in the Eaton's catalogue.

We have hydro now and for our appliances, we got a toaster, iron and the washing machine changed to electric. Danny bought us a string of lights for the tree.

UNTIL 1953, when hydro lines brought light to the Swan River Valley, my parents used oil lamps to chase the shadows to the corners of the house. When the lines were being strung, anyone along the route who wanted to be connected had to have three electrical appliances to qualify. My parents did not have much money, but they purchased an iron, a toaster with sides that flipped down to allow bread to be placed in it, and a motor for Mum's ringer washing machine. When the wires along the road went live, single-bulb light fixtures were wired into the house. At one special Christmas, Lynette, who was nearsighted, got a reading lamp under the tree. Large appliances, such as a refrigerator or an electric stove, were out of my parents' price range, along with a water heater or an electric furnace.

My memory of the house is of constant chill unless we were in the kitchen where Mum cooked and the wood stove radiated warmth. In the winter, Daddy put a contraption that looked like a large stovepipe on legs in the older part of the house to warm the bedrooms. The "heater" could be a deathtrap for the unsuspecting. The unprotected heat source could get glass melting hot and "do not touch" rang in my ears daily. On the upside, the cold house meant food rarely spoiled in the winter and we could have ice cream that never melted. Mum made the custard and Daddy gathered icicles from along the eaves, breaking them into useable chunks to fit between the custard container and the wooden barrel of the ice cream freezer. We took turns cranking the gears to keep the canister turning so the contents would freeze evenly. As the ice cream froze, it became harder to turn the crank and then Daddy would take over to finish it. We enjoyed every flavour Mum devised. In particular, we loved her pumpkin ice cream that tasted like pie without the crust.

With no means to keep food frozen through a hot summer, ice cream was mostly a winter treat for us. I remember one day in early summer when Daddy climbed down the cribbing in the well to gather ice to make ice cream for us. The sheltered dark well had maintained ice later than usual that year. Terrified he would fall and drown in the well, I had to be taken back to the house to ease my anxiety. Perhaps after so many cautions to stay away from wells, I couldn't understand why he would willingly climb down inside one.

Mum cooked non-stop and her kitchen remained hot no matter the season. She also sewed most of our clothes, maintained a large garden, washed and ironed, and got us off to school with full lunch pails and completed homework. She operated a two-tier pressure cooker/canner in summer and, during the winter, we ate two-quart jars of meat, vegetables, and fruit she had "put up." She made countless jars of jam, jelly, and pickles. We rarely ate food we did not produce on the farm, but large tins of peanut butter that had to be stirred when opened to get the oil distributed evenly through it were a store-bought staple. Tins of headcheese, which supplied Mum with pans in which to bake bread, and many pounds of bologna and countless tins of sardines were inexpensive sources of protein we purchased at the Bowsman Co-op store.

From a child's-eye view, life couldn't be grander. I happily played with my farm animals, Naomi Catherine, and imaginary friends. I loved to be read to and I could often persuade a sibling or parent to read me "one chapter." I also wanted to be helpful. Mum would let me decorate cookies, knead bits of bread dough, or sprinkle sugar and cinnamon on leftover pie crust she baked into a yummy treat. She recited nursery rhymes to me as she kneaded dough and sang along with music on the radio. Being included in whatever activities occurred in our world made me feel loved and important.

The house, especially after the addition of the kitchen, became our haven. Even in winter's cold, there couldn't be a better place to be. We sat around the heater in the evenings and Daddy would read to us while Mum knitted, crocheted, or mended our clothes. My parents must have been in constant worry over how they would make ends meet. Would the sale of eggs or chickens or cream net enough extra cash to send an order to the Eaton's catalogue for the gifts Santa Claus would deliver? My parents worked tirelessly to bring the magic of Christmas into our lives, from serving our Christmas morning milk in mugs with Santa's face on them to creating an Advent calendar out of connected rings of construction paper. We excitedly tore off a link every day in the run-up to the twenty-fifth. On Christmas morning, our delight at finding our stockings full of wonderful treats and a mandarin orange in the toe must have given them joy. In my memory, "Santa's" generosity could only be eclipsed by the magic created by the lights on the tree we meticulously decorated on Christmas Eve.

The house surrounded us, and coming home to it made me feel safe. Daddy took good care of his family, getting up in the pre-dawn cold to stoke the fire in the wood stove and heater before heading to the animal-warmed barn to do the morning milking and feeding. By the time he got back to the house with pails of milk to separate, Mum would have breakfast started and the house would be warming up. Then it would be time for Edward, Lynette, and me to get up and prepare for our days.

Getting up in a cold house is uncomfortable; it's an unpleasant experience I retain from my childhood. I don't know how Daddy did it day after day in the winter. Of course, when you are in charge of animals, you can't stay in bed. Daddy had been getting up in the cold his entire life and had survived primitive conditions during the war, so he likely never thought about the comfort of putting his feet on a warm floor. I prefer to stay in bed where it is warm if I know getting up will introduce me to cold air. Even though I now live in one of the coldest cities in the country, it is indoor cold I dislike. If my house is unexpectedly cold when I come in from outside, I feel the same stress as I did when entering the farmhouse after the fire had been out for several hours on a winter's night.

In summer, the house absorbed the warmth from the sun. It didn't have windows that opened easily to allow for cross breezes and the heat became stifling. With no electric stove, the wood stove remained stoked all day. Mum regularly baked bread, and three meals a day were prepared on the hot range. Daddy liked dessert at the end of a meal, which meant an endless number of pies, cakes, and cookies exited the wood-heated oven. The cookies found their way into our lunches along with sandwiches made with her perfect bread.

Mum loved variety and we never suffered the monotony of white bread day after day. She would sometimes ask me what kind of bread she should make and I always asked for oatmeal. In my childish opinion, no other snack beat home-churned butter on a slice of fresh oatmeal bread. I use her oatmeal bread recipe today, but it never tastes as wonderful as when she made it. A professional cook might suggest that my flour is different from what

Mum used or that she used her own churned butter and I am using store-bought or, *gasp*, margarine. I prefer the explanation provided by a friend who told me "the love is missing."

Mum didn't have time to sit and entertain me during the day because she had dozens of chores to do between sun up and after nightfall. I sat on our metal stool beside the table to watch her mix the bread dough. After kneading it into a perfectly smooth ball, she left it to rise in the warming oven above the stove. She would give me a portion of the dough and show me how to knead it and shape it. My siblings had the same task when they were preschool age. I think she baked our "bread" along with the rest of the batch and we presented it to our father for his approval. I don't remember giving him my grubby well-kneaded offerings, but Lynette recalls his exclamations of delight over getting "brown" bread when the rest of the family got white!

Despite the double heat from summer temperatures and the working wood stove, I don't remember us ever eating anywhere but at the wooden table that sat in the kitchen. We didn't have a deck, or what is commonly known now as an "outdoor room," and we didn't have television, so all our meals were eaten together. In their youth, my parents enjoyed picnics with friends and we often had family picnics with our grandparents and cousins, but we never left the hot kitchen in the summer to eat our meal outside in the unkempt front yard. Perhaps the effort of carrying everything out and then back in again put a damper on that activity for Mum. So we ate at the table that a few hours before would have been scattered with flour, baking pans, various ingredients, such as dried fruit or nuts, and racks cooling the baked result.

After supper, Daddy prepared to head back to the barn for the evening milking and to make sure the animals had all they needed to be comfortable through the night. I could sometimes persuade him to read me the comics, either the funny papers as they arrived in *The Western Producer* or another reread of a comic book that belonged to one of us. A huge fan of *Dennis the Menace,* Daddy sometimes brought me a *Dennis the Menace* comic book if he had made a trip to town. The year before I started school, I got a *Dennis the Menace* school kit that had a little leather book bag, a notebook, a ruler, a pencil, and an eraser. I couldn't wait to start school! Daddy may have looked forward to my learning to read. Or maybe he enjoyed our little game of my standing in front of him with a comic tucked behind my back.

"Oh, and what have you there?" he would ask. When I revealed my hidden treasure, he would weakly insist he needed to get to the barn. In the end, I always won and he would read two panels of my choosing or two pages of a comic book.

I shadowed Daddy everywhere. I had a small rubber pail that I took to the beach, to pick blueberries in, and to water my squash seeds that Mum helped me plant. But, in Daddy's company, I carried that pail filled with chop so I could help feed the pigs. He carried his two large pails full of feed and dumped them over the fence into the trough. The excited pigs would shove and push each other to reach the food. With that done, Daddy helped me. He would lift me to the top of the fence and I would pour my small offering in the direction of the trough. It usually fell onto the heads of the eating pigs.

With no electrical supply, water could not be pumped to the animals. The cows spent much of their time on pasture that had a pond or were funnelled to our dugout for water. For calves, chickens, pigs, horses, and animals that needed to be near the barn, water troughs had to be topped up daily. Daddy hand-hauled water from the well that used a pulley system, not a pump, filling large pails that he carried to the troughs. It could take several trips unless heavy rain had supplemented the water supply. Of course, I helped. He put water in my little pail and we would head across the yard to the corral and empty our containers into the trough. My contribution amounted to a thimbleful in comparison to his Niagara Falls of water! As long as I heeded his warnings to not get close to the back ends of the horses or cows, I could follow him everywhere. Mum said he loved having me with him.

"He'd come in from the barn and tell me to get you dressed because he had to go to town," Mum told me. While he changed into cleaner clothes to go to Bowsman for chick feed or to see if a cream or egg cheque had arrived, she would dress me in an outfit she made and style my natural curls into Shirley Temple-style ringlets. Folks in town got used to seeing my tall, dark-haired, tanned father walking hand-in-hand with his fair-skinned, blond youngest child. Jovial and outgoing, he visited with everyone he met. I imagine he would scoop me into his arms when I got tired while he indulged in a chin-wag in the Co-op store or the elevator. I don't think I was spoiled because he could be very strict, but I think I was indulged.

I wonder where Daddy learned his loving behaviour. I certainly can't imagine my Grandma Tennison cuddling her oldest child. My mother's parents were kind and loving, but farming is a full-time job with endless overtime, so I don't know how many hours they had to devote to hands-on childcare. Daddy may have instinctively understood a child's need to be loved or he may have observed how his future in-laws interacted with their children as he watched Mum grow up.

WILDWOOD

Naomi and Dan standing in front of their parents on the front steps of Wildwood on their wedding day in 1947. Standing behind them, from left to right: Harley and Iva Bradley, Agnes and George Tennison.

Harley's coin was the closest. Both the northeast and northwest quarters had prospects of roads. Harley had not seen much of the section but he chose the northeast quarter... At the Claims Office, they each gave their ten dollars and got a permit to live on the land and do their duties. They also had to be naturalized sometime. [The men] loaded their trunk on the next train and went to Bowsman River to start a new life.

From Harley Bradley's account of homesteading, as told to Rosalie

WILDWOOD. THE NAME my maternal grandparents, Iva and Harley Bradley, gave their property aptly describes the stands of trees filled with cranberry, saskatoon, and chokecherry bushes that we picked from every summer. Like *Citizen Kane's* nostalgic memories of Rosebud, the word Wildwood has me thinking of laughter and happy times. In the late 1960s, Grandma hired a neighbour, who was trying to earn a little money with her talent, to paint a sign depicting the house and gardens with "Welcome to Wildwood" carefully lettered on it. Grandpa installed the artistry on posts at the end of the long lane, inviting everyone to their home.

Viewed from the main road, the house stood elegantly on a slight rise surrounded by a manicured lawn and a flower garden horseshoe that never lacked colour for the duration of the summer. Grandpa and Grandma planted what became a majestic stand of spruce trees along the lane that guided visitors to the grey stucco home. Hidden by the treed lane, the farmyard with its matching garage and machine shed, some older unused log outbuildings, and a three-section wooden granary completed the property we called the home farm. In the middle of the great farmyard, a small enclosure hid the well. (Visitors kept mistaking it for the outhouse, so Grandpa painted "Well, well, water!" on it.) Behind the buildings, a slough surrounded by trees gave shelter and water to cattle, horses, deer, and other wildlife. Fields of waving grain in the summer and snow in the winter stretched along the lane, presenting an unbroken view of the house.

But, before my grandparents made Wildwood one of the most prominent houses in what eventually became known as the McKay District, hard work carved it out of the Manitoba wilderness.

Harley Edward Bradley of Whitehouse, Ohio, willingly turned his hand to a variety of jobs. This entrepreneurial spirit sustained him when he became a farmer. As a boy, he worked for fifty cents a day to thin beets, but it cost him five cents to get a ride to the field. His parents bought him a pony and he cultivated gardens for his neighbours. After graduating from high school in 1911, he and a cousin started buying and selling chickens, cream, and fruit in Whitehouse. He and a friend dug and ground horseradish they preserved with vinegar and sold to a local store for five cents a jar. Eventually, he took jobs on the big boats plying the Great Lakes out of Toledo, working as a coal passer, a watchman, and, eventually, a porter. When his younger sister (his only sibling) died, he returned to Whitehouse, getting a job in a tin shop owned by a friend.

Harley, like many young men, wanted adventure. One evening, he and three friends heard a Canadian land agent extol the virtues of life in western Canada. According to Grandpa, a person could get a quarter section (160 acres) of land for ten dollars and if, within a three-year period, they "made good" on the property, their ten-spot would be refunded. Making good meant clearing enough land to grow a crop or to sustain cattle and spending at least six months each year living on their quarter in some form of permanent shelter.

"It was like betting us ten dollars against 160 acres that we could not do that while fighting mosquitoes, bulldogs, bed bugs, heel flies for cattle, nose flies for horses, and no-see-ums," Grandpa told me in 1975 when I asked about his early life in Canada for a history project. He never imagined that the greatest challenge to his success would be thousands of annoying insects.

In August 1913, Harley and his friends travelled by train from Detroit, Michigan, to Windsor, Ontario, and then on to Dauphin, Manitoba, in search of adventure and "free" land. The over 4,400-kilometre trip cost roughly seventeen dollars. But, when they arrived in Dauphin, there was no land option that interested them. They boarded the train again and continued north to the Swan River Valley, another two hundred kilometres.

When they got to the town of Swan River, they learned that most of the land had already been settled. An old gentleman they met told them they needed to go farther north to Bowsman River, where there were still parcels to be had. They arranged transportation to a section of land they were told was "only suitable for growing frogs." The untouched wilderness had sandy soil and lots of trees.

"We made up our minds this was where we were going to settle," Grandpa told me as he relaxed in an easy chair in Wildwood's living room. "We turned around and made the journey back to town to stake our claim." Even though the distance was only about fifty kilometres, with a horse and wagon and walking around the untouched tract of land, the excursion took all day.

Back in Swan River, they drew a line in the dirt in front of the Claims Office and each threw a twenty-five-cent piece at it. The closest to the line got first choice of the quarters on section 21. Harley won the coin toss and he chose the northeast quarter—21-38-25—because it held the prospect of two roads. After a year or two of struggle on their homesteads, the others moved back to the United States and easier ways to make a living. But Grandpa stayed and made a new life as a farmer. Did he ever get his ten dollars back? No, but he told me when he started getting Canada's Old Age Pension, he figured the government was returning his investment with interest.

The men built a small cabin they shared in the centre of the section close to each man's quarter. The four friends cleared land during the day and played endless games of euchre at night. They hunted for food, learning to cook wild game and make use of local berries. Grandpa eventually got a Purity Flour cookbook that he hung on a nail with a loop of string. The cookbook is grubby and worn from years of use, but I pull it off my shelf occasionally looking for Grandpa's recipe for popcorn balls or headcheese. I have been disappointed when the recipe I seek isn't there. I guess his specialties came from other sources and were memorized after years of use. However, before he got instruction from Purity, he improvised. Hungry for rice pudding, he poured rice, sugar, and milk in a pot and put it in the oven. As the rice expanded, his creation boiled over the sides of the pot. He quickly scooped up the excess, transferred it to another pot, added more milk, and put both pots back in the oven. He said he ate that pudding for many days, learning he didn't need to use quite so much rice.

When Grandpa decided to stay in Canada, he wanted a house of his own. Climbing a tall spruce tree, he surveyed his property. He noticed an area that had been burnt by fire and decided it would be the easiest spot on which to build his first log home and outbuildings. Wildwood began to take shape.

Many of the men needed to find work away from their homestead in order to have enough money to continue their farming operation the following year. Grandpa worked at another farm as a labourer on the threshing crew. Meanwhile, another immigrant from the United States, Elmer Epler, settled on land not far from Harley's homestead and began raising cattle rather than crops. To support his enterprise, he got a winter job with a logging company. He asked his mother, Katie Epler, and youngest sister to travel to Canada from Pennsylvania to help. In November 1914, my great-granny Epler and my future grandmother Frances Iva Epler (known as Iva) found themselves on an isolated homestead caring for Elmer's animals. At sixteen, Grandma was one of very few single young women in the area.

Survival in the early days of the twentieth century, with little money and no Gore-Tex or lined boots in a rugged, sometimes unforgiving, landscape, challenged the homesteaders. During the long, cold, dark winter, when the women needed flour or feed chopped for the cattle, they spent a day shovelling grain into a wagon. In the predawn of the next morning, Iva hitched the horses to the wagon and left the yard for the twenty-four-kilometre drive to the elevator in Bowsman River (the name was eventually shortened to Bowsman) to get the grain ground. Upon arrival in the town, she joined the queue of wagons waiting their turn at the elevator. The men would take pity on the young girl and watch her horses while she went into the office to get warm. With her ground grain loaded back on the wagon, she began the return trip. With only about seven hours of daylight during the winter months, she made the majority of the trip in the dark. When she arrived back on the homestead, the dog barked a welcome. When he heard the dog, William Ferguson, a bachelor who lived on the neighbouring homestead, would run over and send her to the warmth of the cabin while he unhitched her horses and put them in the barn for the night. Stiff with cold, Iva said she couldn't take her boots and outer clothing off without help.

My grandparents were always coy about when or how they met. It's possible the homesteaders gathered for evenings of music or to share gossip or just to be in contact with another person. But on a cold day at the end of January in 1919, Harley and Iva made the long trip to Bowsman to get married.

Grandma gave birth to Uncle Henry in August, which explains why they needed to brave the elements to get married on the coldest day in January. My mother, Naomi, arrived in November 1920. By this time, my grandparents were living in a two-storey log home on Grandpa's homestead. When we visited their farm during my childhood, only the second storey of the home remained. Mum never failed to tell me: "This is the house I was born in."

Harley and Iva were hard workers. While he developed the farm, she created a home. Grandma sewed and knitted for the family, and she cooked anything Grandpa brought home, from fish to moose. Together, they prospered, until tough times hit around 1925, when the price for cattle plummeted. Grandpa decided the family should move in search of a better income. They rented out the farm and moved to his hometown of Whitehouse, Ohio. Grandpa found a job and Grandma started a business weaving and selling rugs. The move wasn't as successful as they'd hoped because Grandpa developed a lung condition while they lived in Whitehouse and his doctor told him to go back to Canada's better air. By then, they had four children—Henry, Naomi, and Irene (Rene), born in Canada before they moved, and William (Billie), born in Ohio. Packing as much as possible in their Flint touring car, the family prepared to head north. Using earnings from her rug business, Grandma had bought an upright Ellington grand piano and she wouldn't leave it behind. They added a trailer to their caravan to carry the piano, Grandma's loom, and other possessions they had acquired, including two Maine Coon cats, and headed north. In 1929, they arrived back at Wildwood, where they became influential in the district.

My grandparents were generous and kind. When we were at Wildwood, we wanted for nothing and they had time to talk to a child. Iva could be generous to a fault, giving away clothing or household items to someone who needed them more. She once gave away a teapot Mum received as a gift from a friend because a visitor at Wildwood exclaimed over the pot's loveliness. Mum came home from school one day to find her mother cutting apart a large dress. An Ohio friend, Mrs. Lehman, often sent outworn clothing to my grandmother knowing it would be put to good use.

"Are you making me a dress?" Mum asked. "Can I have a bow on it?"

"No, I'm making dresses for the Brown girls. They can't go to school because they don't have anything to wear," my grandmother replied.

"But I need a new dress."

"No, you don't. I'll add a piece to your blue dress to make it longer. It will get you through the summer," Iva explained. "Elsie and Myrtle have one dress to share and that's why they can only go to school on alternate days." Throughout her life, Grandma helped anyone who needed a meal or an item of clothing, sometimes at the expense of her own family.

Equally generous, but with an authoritarian streak that could be a help or a hindrance depending on the situation, Grandpa ruled his family with a sternness that cowed my mother. While she loved her father, Mum did not thrive under his direction. He didn't take time to consider the consequences his decisions might have on her. Other family members ably ignored his dictatorial style.

A high school graduate, Grandpa wanted his children to be educated. He sent them to the McKay School, a one-room school for all the children in the district that he helped initiate. My grandparents often boarded the teacher, and Grandpa served with the group overseeing the school's operation. Grandpa lobbied to get the main road that stretched from one end of the district to the other, passing by Wildwood, graded and gravelled. He took names on petitions to get hydro and telephone to the area and actively raised money to support the local branch of the Farmers' Union. Grandma, a longtime member of the Lenswood Women's Institute, helped organize entertainment, such as variety concerts, and hosted quilting bees.

According to Mum, the family survived the Great Depression because they had a farm. Their huge garden and Grandpa's proficiency at hunting and fishing kept them all fed. Eventually, Uncle Henry did much of the hunting and fishing and became a respected trapper. They got through the Depression on grit and ingenuity.

Grandma did her best to provide nutrition and comfort to her children. The family picked berries throughout the summer, making jam and jelly, if they could get sugar. Grandpa smoked fish and meat to preserve them. He traded his smoked goldeye at a general store in Bowsman for items, such as salt or sugar, that they couldn't grow or manufacture themselves. Once she re-purposed secondhand clothes sent from relatives and friends into dresses and shirts for family and friends, Grandma used small remnants of the fabric to make quilts.

"I'm bored" was not a phrase spoken by my grandparents' children, because something always needed to be done. Items in Grandma's knitting basket—a sock, a scarf—had to be completed and the children were told to pick up the needles instead of complaining or sitting idle. They spun wool shorn from their own sheep into yarn and then knitted it into items to keep them warm while they walked to school eating rosehips along the way, not knowing they were replenishing their vitamin C.

My mother's and aunt's educations did not end when they finished Grade 9 by correspondence at McKay School. With no buses to pick them up for the twenty-four-kilometre trek to the nearest school in Bowsman, they would need to move to town, pay for room and board with another family, and fund tuition. My grandparents could not afford that cost in the 1930s. Instead the sisters were sent to Pennsylvania for high school. A dual citizen born in Canada to American parents, Mum could travel between the two countries freely. Their good friends the Lehmans, who made the trip back and forth annually, gave Mum a ride to her family in Pennsylvania. Her aunts, Grandma's half-sisters, happily took her in. Her dual citizenship meant she could attend high school with her cousins and not pay tuition.

Painfully shy, Mum compensated for her timidness by becoming a perfectionist. She reasoned that, if she did everything perfectly, she could not be chastised for or be embarrassed by mistakes. The high school she went to had a secretarial program, and Mum excelled at it. The principal assigned her to assist his secretary with the daily work in the office, giving her much needed experience. Mum graduated from Elizabethtown High School in 1939. I wonder if she might have stayed in the United States had Grandpa not ordered her home. During her three years in the United States, she made friends, had small jobs that gave her some independence and cash, and there were hints of a budding romance. But in Mum's last year of high school, her younger sister, Irene, arrived to start her education. My aunt was born after my grandparents became naturalized Canadian citizens and, as such, she had to report to Canada every year. Mum wanted to stay in Pennsylvania. But Grandpa decreed that since Auntie Rene had to return to Canada in the summer of 1939 and a ride had been found for her, Mum should come home as well. She complied.

Mum returned to Canada just before Europe erupted in war. She came home to isolation on the farm and no hope of a job unless she moved to an urban location. Mum rekindled her friendship with Daddy and, when he went to Winnipeg to train for the military, he asked her to come to the big city. Many of her friends were in Winnipeg to be close to sweethearts, and they worked at the department stores or in the houses of the city's elite. Mum could not find a secretarial position but, with the help of friends, got a job as a maid for a wealthy Winnipeg family. Thrilled to have money after the privations of the previous decade, she was awed by the abundance of goods available at Eaton's and the Hudson's Bay Company. According to Mum, after years of use and no money for replacements, there wasn't a single piece of crockery in her parents' log cabin that didn't have a chip or a crack. With some of her first wages, she bought her mother a set of dishes at Eaton's and had the store ship the package to Bowsman. During the previous winter, Mum and Grandma had shared an overcoat, so another purchase was a warm outer garment for the coming cold weather.

On her days off, she met Daddy and they went to the movies. Her active social life included meeting friends for picnics and double dating with Daddy and his friends. Working as a maid may not have been Mum's dream job, especially when one of her employers refused to pay her. A family friend got her money by threatening the disagreeable boss and she moved on to work for a much nicer family.

Mum enjoyed the freedom of life in the big city, but it ended too soon. Daddy shipped out to England on his personal march toward war and Mum received a letter from Grandpa.

*[We] built another log house but this one was well finished
on the inside and stuccoed on the outside. At this time
Henry was serving in the army with the Winnipeg Rifles
but Billie... and Naomi were still at home to help.*

*[I] canvassed the neighbourhood to find out how many
would like telephones in their homes and, in 1947, phones
were added to the homes... [We] had electricity installed...
and the power was turned on in time for Christmas. By this
time, Henry was home from overseas and did the wiring.
Henry also put running water in the house.*

From Harley Bradley's account of
homesteading, as told to Rosalie

WHEN CANADA joined the Allied defence against aggression in Europe, prices for agricultural products increased. As their prosperity grew, my grandparents decided they wanted a new house. Grandpa wrote to Mum telling her to come home because they needed help. Her compliant attitude kept her under his thumb and she never developed the fortitude to stand up to him, so she returned to Wildwood. While bowing to his wishes eventually led to the creation of a safe haven for me, I wonder how different her life would have been had she refused his summons. He might have been angry, but likely wouldn't have made the long trek to Winnipeg to bring her forcibly home.

Through 1942 and 1943, Mum worked alongside her younger brother Billie and Grandpa to dig a basement for a new house using shovels and a wheelbarrow to take the dirt out of the hole. It must have been hard, dirty work. With the hole dug, Grandpa poured a cement basement. A new two-storey log house rose on the foundation. They spent many hours chinking the logs on the interior to make a smooth surface for the application of Gyproc. A man known locally as Stucco John came and coated the exterior with grey stucco.

The nicest in the neighbourhood, my grandparent's house became the centre of our lives and the surrounding community's. The extensive flower gardens were visited often by people from around the province. Every summer, Grandpa and Grandma invited the residents of the seniors' home in Swan River to come and enjoy the garden. My cousins and I were called on to serve tea, coffee, strawberries, and ice cream to the visitors after they finished the tour.

The house Mum helped dig the basement for became my second home and the mansion of my childhood. I knew every nook and cranny, including the secret loose floorboard in Mum's room, under which she hid her treasures.

In the summer, the family played baseball in the big farmyard and hide-and-seek at dusk. Grandpa made us kites and taught us how to fly them. In the winter, we played fox and geese in the untouched snow in a corner of the yard. If cold or rain kept us indoors, we played board games at the big oak table. I challenged Grandpa at crokinole in the evenings, and he taught me to play euchre. If any of the cousins got a new game for Christmas, they would bring it to the farm for us all to learn.

Grandma Tennison lived in Ontario from 1948 until her death in 1971, and I only have vague and not very pleasant memories of her. But my mother's parents, Harley and Iva, were ever present in my life. Daddy adored his mother-in-law and would do anything she asked of him, including stopping along the road to dig plants she wanted for her garden. With no other side of the family to compete with, my family spent every major holiday at Mum's parents' farm and we were frequently there for Sunday dinners.

I shadowed Grandpa whenever we visited Wildwood. One day, as teenage me helped him with a project I no longer remember, he offered some sage advice about boys: "Y'know, Sis (a nickname he used for most females in the family), I always took the measure of a man by how he treated his horses." While I lived in a rural community and many families had horses, I had no idea how the boys I knew from school might handle animals in their care. A local rodeo supplied a crowd of men with horses and, at the time, I wondered if Grandpa thought I should date a cowboy. From the distance of many years, I realize he was trying to tell me that a man who mistreats a horse would also mistreat people. He overlooked that, in my world, most boys drove cars and I would have no opportunity to see how they might interact with animals.

At my grandparents' house I saw my first television shows. We watched *The Ed Sullivan Show*, *Hazel*, and *The Beverly Hillbillies*. We saw the funeral of John F. Kennedy on their black and white set in 1963. I didn't understand whose funeral we were watching or why the adults around me were so sad. After events that rocked my family in 1964, I'd remember the young Kennedy children watching their father's casket pass by and feel a kinship with them.

Large built-in cabinets showcased Grandma's collection of bone china cups and saucers and the twelve place settings of ironstone we used at every special family dinner. Unlike our farmhouse, Wildwood had many electrical appliances—an electric stove (in addition to a wood stove), a refrigerator, a double-wide freezer, a television, movie and slide projectors, an electric sewing machine, plus many smaller appliances.

Grandpa and Grandma had indoor plumbing! When my grandparents planned Wildwood, they didn't overlook a single detail, including a septic system along with backup options to protect it. In summer, we were encouraged to use the rather luxurious outhouse instead of running upstairs to the flush toilet. Unlike many outhouses that were hammered together out of scrap lumber, Grandpa had built a sturdy one tucked into some trees at the back of the yard. Painted to co-ordinate with the house, it had two adult holes and a smaller, shorter hole tucked into a corner. When I graduated from the children's hole to the adult holes, I felt so grown up! In the winter, Grandpa installed a chemical toilet in the basement to reduce stress on the straw-covered septic system and save us from frostbitten trips through the snow to the bathroom in the trees. I liked to visit the bathroom in the house just to look at its matching fixtures, cupboard for towel storage, and coordinating shower and window curtains. I'd never seen a room like it in any other house.

My grandparents planned the house for maximum efficiency. The two upstairs bedrooms and a smaller half room were tucked under the roof line creating an angled ceiling on one side of each room—a hazard for a tall person sitting up in bed at night. Storage cupboards below the angle hid all sorts of magical items, including Christmas decorations, old quilts and clothing, and boxes of fabric and ribbons. Grandma's half-sisters worked in clothing factories in Pennsylvania and they bought excess cotton fabric and trim to send her. The fabric her sisters sent found its way into quilts or became a dress or a shirt for a grandchild. My great-aunts sent boxes of buttons that were divided between the sewers in the family for use on shirts or as eyes on stuffed toys. Occasionally, boxes of trim would arrive that Grandma used to decorate aprons she donated to the Women's Institute sales. She trimmed dresses for her granddaughters with yards of rickrack or decorative woven tape.

A cupboard built beside the landing three-quarters of the way up the stairs held many mysteries. Mum once revealed a hint of its secrets to me when we sat on the landing and she removed a small box containing a pair of small pearl-handled pistols. She said they were gifts Grandma received from a relative. I don't know if they had ever been fired. I imagined my Grandma brandishing one of the pistols to save herself from the advances of a nefarious roué. In reality, they would be useless protection on a remote farm threatened mostly by coyotes. I have no idea what other secrets that cupboard hid because snooping through closets, even in the home of family, is "the height of bad manners."

The smaller half bedroom was sometimes occupied by the hired girl or the teacher. When the room was unoccupied, Grandma used it for a craft studio. Interested in the natural world, Grandma collected items to satisfy her curiosity and expand her knowledge. She amassed a large collection of shells gathered or bought during her and Grandpa's frequent trips. She identified and labelled the shells and displayed them on shelves and in frames built by Grandpa. A willing grandchild would be put to work painting or gluing as she constructed people and creatures out of varying shapes and sizes of shells. We all have pelicans, Santa Claus figures, and imaginative creatures weighted with plaster of Paris so they won't tip over. Grandma's greatest achievement was "The Shell Wedding." She created a bride, groom, minister, and wedding guests out of shells and housed them in a wooden church Grandpa built to display the tableau. When Grandma or Mum would open the door of the church to let me peer in at the assembly, I imagined Cinderella was marrying her prince.

A large upstairs landing had space for Grandma's sewing desk, built by Grandpa, and a platform rocker that squashed many of our fingers when we played in the space. Along the wall, floor-to-ceiling cupboards stored linens and quilts. A door off the main hall led outside to a platform over the summer kitchen. A clothesline, accessed from the platform and connected to a tall pole in the middle of the lawn, dried sheets and aired quilts. The upper line kept the large items high above anyone crossing the yard. I wasn't allowed on the platform in case I tumbled off the roof. A lower clothesline running from the same tall pole to a shorter one nearer the house was used for drying smaller items.

My grandparents' bedroom was an out-of-bounds room on the main floor and could not be entered without their permission. Grandma kept a cardboard box containing a doll and some clothes, a few plastic dishes, and some toy cars for our amusement in the closet, but we could not retrieve it without asking her first.

In the hall beside the stairs, a wood chair sat near a black rotary dial wall telephone. The hard chair and the party line discouraged long conversations. Tying up the phone or listening to someone else's conversation got the offender reprimanded for their bad manners. Thanks to the party line, the district learned about my family's joys and sorrows before us because not everyone got the bad manners lecture we did. Cautioned not to chat with friends in case someone else needed the line, I would be interrupted by a grandparent or Mum instructing me to hang up if I exceeded their predetermined time limit. Mum pointed out the impoliteness of visiting my grandparents only to spend my time on the telephone with a friend I would see at school in a day or two.

We never lacked for food at my grandparents' house. Years of farm living, deprivation during hard times, and the distance to town meant the basement freezers were full of food. Grandpa and my uncles hunted, filling the freezers with venison and moose, and added variety with fish and the meat of domestic animals. A bountiful summer crop of vegetables and berries—corn, peas, beans, strawberries, saskatoons, blueberries, raspberries, gooseberries—joined ice cream and items with a shorter shelf life, like milk, in the freezer. The shelves sagged with jams, jellies, homemade juice, home-canned fruit, and commercially canned soup that could be turned to in a pinch when the freezer inventory shrank over the winter. Grandpa preserved moose and fish in his smokehouse and the result of his labour hung from hooks in the ceiling giving the room a wonderful smell. Given the job of running downstairs to get a bag of corn out of the freezer, I would linger in the room looking at the abundance of food, pretending I worked in a grocery store.

"Rosalie, where's the corn? Grandma's waiting." Mum's voice would snap me out of my imaginary world and I would scamper up the stairs, completing my errand.

At least one day in late summer many members of the family would go berry picking. Uncle Henry put benches in the back of his grain truck and we would head "over east" to prime blueberry picking grounds. Uncle Henry had a trapline in the area in the 1950s that got burned out in a forest fire. In fact, he nearly burned in the fire. He survived by submerging himself in the creek until the fire jumped it and moved on. Out of disaster comes great goodness sometimes, and the area became fertile for blueberries.

We picked all day, stopping at midday for a picnic lunch. Everyone had to pick. While Uncle Henry, Grandma and Grandpa, Mum, and other adults picked into honey pails or galvanized gallon pails, the children were given smaller pails to ensure quicker gratification and reduce the onset of boredom. Even so, I remember being told I had to keep picking because we could not play until our pails were level full. Each pail of berries got dumped into narrow wooden boxes Grandpa made out of thin spruce slats that sat on the tailgate of the truck. Once full, lids were nailed on the boxes to prevent spillage. We used our now empty pails to play in the sand that surrounded us.

After a full day of picking, we climbed back in the truck, returning to my grandparents' house, where we then had to clean the berries. The boxes were opened and dumped in the centre of the oilcloth-covered table. Using rulers to pull the berries toward us, we removed sticks, leaves, and bugs. The day's picking filled bags for the freezer or glass containers for use in jam and pie. Everyone who showed up for the day shared the picked bounty.

I remember the berry picking excursions as carefree, yet tiring. The days may have been filled with work, mosquitos, sand flies, and heat, but I only remember feeling happy. Decades later, memories of those bucolic berry picking days give my heart a pump of joy.

Surrounding most of my childhood memories is this carefully planned house with all its nooks and crannies and learning opportunities in every corner. I did not recognize Wildwood for the school it was until years later. Living on my own away from Mum and Grandma, I never needed instruction on making quilting templates out of cereal boxes or how to create soup from scratch. I absorbed many lessons just by being in a house populated with clever people I loved being around.

THE FARMHOUSE

Family photo, 1959. From left to right: Edward, Naomi, Dan holding Rosalie, and Lynette.

*Cleaned the big room and
painted the wall green.*

*Danny, Edward and I did the threshing.
It took eight days—1,326 bushels.*

IN MY CHILDHOOD innocence, I didn't notice the stark differences between our farmhouse and Wildwood. Children are happiest, I think, when they feel safe. I certainly was as long as I stayed away from the dugout, the capped wells, and any other hazard that might threaten a child. I didn't mind having to wear socks and slippers to protect my feet from slivers in the cold floors. None of the deprivations we lived with overshadowed my understanding that I was surrounded by a loving family. I probably would have been content to live in the barn as long as we were together.

So, no matter what my family did, I insinuated myself into the action. I don't think I ever saw myself as small.

I determinedly kept up. If I began to lag behind, someone would carry me. I think my parents and siblings were blessed with an abundance of patience because I don't remember them ever telling me "you can't come" or that I couldn't take part in whatever adventure they had planned next.

My parents did their best to make our home comfortable. Sometimes all it took was a new sheet of linoleum or fresh paint. Cost determined which comforts could be undertaken and they likely saved for several months in order to buy needed supplies.

"A lick of paint will spruce up the house," Mum declared one summer. Choosing a leafy green oil paint at the Bowsman Co-op, she and Daddy, Lynette and Edward got to work covering years of accumulated soot from wood fires and lamps that had dulled the finish on the walls. We didn't have paint rollers, so big wide brushes were used to apply the oil paint. Edward and Lynette painted from the floor to their height. Mum and Daddy painted from the ceiling down to meet their efforts. Of course, I insisted on painting as well. A small brush was found and careful instructions, likely by Lynette, guided me on how to apply paint properly. My siblings let me do the bottom of the wall and they painted around me. It didn't take long before I realized they were dripping paint into my hair.

"My hair! It's in my hair!" I squealed. "Stop it!" I was sure they were doing it deliberately. In Edward's case, that was likely true! Now I had a head full of oily green polka dots Mum had trouble removing. But after my initial upset I squeezed between them again wielding my little paint brush.

Our parents believed we should always be learning. Mum started teaching Lynette and Edward to knit and I had to be part of the lesson. I may have been around four. Mum found a broken needle that Daddy sharpened to a point, another size of needle missing its mate, and a leftover ball of thick, bright pink fibre. Mum cast on some stitches and put me to work. Meanwhile, she guided my siblings, who were showing great aptitude. My attempts were not brag-worthy but, when I turned ten, I asked Mum to teach me to knit again. I caught on after only a few mistake-filled rows. I credit my earlier attempt at imprinting the method in my child's brain.

My parents bought my siblings a bicycle—a bright red two-wheeler boy's bike. One would ride the bike to school in the morning and the other would ride it home at night. Or, they would take turns riding from one hydro pole to the next until they turned into our yard. Edward loved riding the bike and he took me with him either on the handlebars or sidesaddle on the centre bar. Happy to be with him, I accepted any suggestion he made regarding our entertainment.

The bicycle proved dangerous to Edward. Once Lynette started high school in Bowsman, Edward had two years of solo time with the bike. As he pedalled home from Craigsford one fall day, he saw my parents threshing in the field. Knowing his help would be welcome, Edward pedalled harder. He hit a rock in the road and flew off the bike over the handlebars, landing on another rock and cutting his leg close to the bone. Bleeding and in pain, he limped toward home pushing the bicycle. Uncle Henry came along in his grain truck, scooped him up, and summoned my parents from the field. Daddy kicked into medic mode, instructing Mum to get an old sheet that he tore into strips to bind Edward's leg. I stood by, afraid something awful had happened to my adored brother. Daddy bundled him into the car and took him to Birch River for Dr. Boon to patch up. Edward had luck on his side. Had the gash been deeper or an inch higher up the leg, the doctor said my brother would likely have had permanent damage to the limb, resulting in a limp or possibly stunted growth.

With Edward hospitalized to ensure his leg healed properly, threshing continued without his help. My parents could not afford a combine and they harvested in the manner my Tennison grandparents had when they travelled west about fifty years earlier. While my Bradley grandparents and neighbours were buying combines in the 1960s, my parents continued to thresh the grain grown on our small, rocky fields. Daddy started early in the morning, after he had done the milking and fed the animals, to thresh our crop. The process would have been easier if he had money to hire help. Instead, he hitched Rusty and Jumbo to the hayrack and headed to the field to collect the stooked sheaves, gritting his teeth every time he had to raise his arms above his aching shoulders to heft the bundles of grain over his head. The well-trained horses plodded along the row of stooks and, when Daddy finished adding the sheaves to the rack, he yelled "gid-dup" and they moved forward to the next stook. He never had to steer them until they got to the end of the field and needed to turn. When the rack was stacked so high with sheaves that Daddy couldn't reach the pinnacle with his pitchfork anymore, the horses hauled it to the clearing where the threshing machine sat.

Mum would get Edward and Lynette off to school and then go to the field to help Daddy. Of course, she had to take me along. The threshing machine connected to the tractor via a seventy-foot loop of heavy canvas and I had great fun bouncing on it. The belt became a bucking horse and, in my mind, our local rodeo had a new star. My parents could see me from the field as long as I stayed by the threshing machine in the clearing. If I got tired, I could sit on the ground under the belt, but I was never to wander off. When they had a rack full of sheaves, they came to the clearing and I would relinquish my seat on the belt so the threshing could continue. While they pitched the sheaves onto the threshing machine conveyor,

I sat out of harm's way, watching the action. Mum lived in fear that I would get caught in the belt. She told me many times how she remembered such an incident in the movie *The Drylanders*, starring Frances Hyland. Having a small child in close proximity to something so dangerous must have worried them but, as long as I stayed where they could see me, they continued the work of getting our crop harvested.

When my siblings were due home from school, my parents would take a break. Mum returned to the house to meet them. Lynette took over my care and helped prepare supper. Edward might go out to take Mum's place on the threshing crew or complete other chores, such as chopping wood to fill the wood box by the stove. If rain threatened, Mum might leave Lynette in charge of me and supper so she and Edward could join Daddy in the field to get as much threshed as possible. If a downpour began soaking the stooks, all threshing stopped. Edward's biking accident reduced the help that year by one, leaving only Mum and Daddy to finish our harvest.

With the grain threshed, Daddy stored it in wooden granaries he built. When the time came to ship our crop through an elevator in Bowsman, he asked Uncle Henry to deliver it in his truck. Daddy always intended to pay for this service, but we suspect he rarely did. With mounting debt, my parents sank deeper into a hole and we did without modern equipment and conveniences. We didn't know what we were missing unless we visited neighbours or relatives and were invited to admire their new tractor or automatic washing machine.

Even in the early 1960s, most farm folk used their machinery until it wore out and then mined it for parts. A new car purchase in the neighbourhood became an event because, back then, vehicles weren't changed on a three-year rotation; they were replaced only when they could no longer be fixed. The same held true for household conveniences. Our relatives or neighbours may have had running water, but they saved it for a weekly bath or washing dishes. In good weather, outhouses saved precious water from being used to flush an indoor toilet.

In our farmhouse, we washed in basins and galvanized tubs that doubled as rinsing receptacles when Mum did laundry with the ringer washer. For the other stuff, we went outside to the outhouse, a short walk from the house and hidden in some trees. In the winter and for nighttime emergencies, we had a bucket with a lid in my parents' bedroom. I don't know who emptied the bucket daily, but one day I had to "go" and someone hadn't done their duty. I didn't like the icky feeling of my bum touching the accumulated urine of my family members. Perhaps we all had high immunity from living in such close quarters and sharing everything!

As a member of the Women's Institute, Mum followed the group's guidance on food safety and she became very conscious of cleanliness and food-borne bacteria.

Cooked meat had no pink showing and she scoured her work surfaces before she baked or prepared food. The only gastrointestinal issues I remember having were acquired elsewhere. During one shopping trip to town, my parents bought us Cheezies as a treat to share on the drive home. But I over-ate and threw up on the rug as soon as I stepped through the door of the house. To this day I don't eat cheese-flavoured snacks!

Our family worked together like the parts of Daddy's well-oiled threshing machine. As the smallest, I couldn't be left alone, so jobs were found to keep me in sight. I might be instructed to pick up the binder twine cut from the sheaves during threshing so the cows or horses wouldn't accidentally eat it. I learned at a very young age how to set the table for meals. Always wanting to be part of the action, I asked for jobs. If the chore was too big or complex for a small child, I became the able assistant, holding the washed sheets above the ground so Mum could pin them to the line. I have no resentment that I worked when I could be playing. I think children who grow up on farms learn instinctively they can contribute to the success of the operation. Sometimes I may have been more of a hindrance than a help but, if my family included me in a project, I gamely followed their instructions.

*Danny and Edward stayed at home
with lots of food that I left for them.*

O N SUNDAYS, after Daddy finished chores, we went to St. Paul's Anglican Church in Bowsman, where he pitched in to light the fire to warm the building in winter and did maintenance in the summer. Daddy built a manger out of willow sticks for the Christmas pageant. He supplied sheaves for the Harvest Home service because only he still threshed.

I attended Sunday School in a tiny room beside the altar that also served as the sacristy. After church, we might be invited for lunch at the homes of friends. Often, these were older people who had sold their farms and moved to town. I was christened in the tiny St. Paul's Anglican church with my parents and a very proper English lady, Mrs. Bea George, listed as godparents. We often went to Auntie Bea's for tea after church.

Occasionally, we went to my grandparents' or to the homes of friends for an afternoon and evening visit. We never stayed late because Daddy had to get home to do chores. Farm families didn't go on vacation because animals needed daily care. On long summer nights, after the cows were milked and the animals fed, we might drive through the gathering dusk to see a movie at the drive-in theatre outside Swan River. Or, we would go to a lake for the day, meeting Grandpa and Grandma and the rest of our family for a picnic.

One autumn, my grandparents planned a trip to Flin Flon for Grandma to learn to make pottery from a woman teaching classes in her home. Mum, Lynette, and I were invited along. This was a very big deal for us as we were not accustomed to being away and staying in the home of strangers. Mum hadn't travelled anywhere since her honeymoon. Daddy and Edward stayed behind to look after the farm. Before he married Mum, Daddy had been a bachelor for many years, capably cooking for himself and managing his own clothing care. Some of his domestic tricks he'd learned while in the army. Nevertheless, there had to have been discussion on whether we should join the trip, how long we would be gone, and what Mum needed to do in advance to ease Daddy's increased workload.

Excited by the prospect of a holiday, I got a place of honour sitting between my grandparents in the front seat of their massive dark-red Plymouth. Those were the days of big cars, bench seats, and no seatbelts. I perched on one of Grandpa's handcrafted footstools so I could see over the dash. Yes, there was a danger of my flying through the windshield in an accident, but I don't remember us meeting any cars on the road to Flin Flon. Grandpa made the long road trip fun, singing me nonsense songs. My favourite ditty, "The Old Hen," Grandpa's uncle had sung to him in the 1800s. I begged him to sing it again and again and I loudly belted out the chorus. I bet Grandma, Mum, and Lynette wished for some quiet in the car while we sang:

> I'll sing you a song, it's not very long about an old hen what is dead
>
> She used to go round a-scratching the ground and this is what she always said:
>
> Rook tooky tooky took took tooky took took took
> That's what she said all the while.
>
> One day she went out a-scratching about I guess she was putting on style
>
> She spread out her tail like a ship with a sail and this is what she said all the while:
>
> Rook tooky tooky took took tooky took took took
> That's what she said all the while.
>
> One day a man come with a two-barrelled gun and said I will fix that old chick
>
> He aimed at her head with a big chunk of lead and that old hen she got sick.
>
> Rook tooky tooky took took tooky took took took
> That's what she said all the while.

> Now that was the end of that funny old hen, she died with a head what was sore
> She folded her wings and I bet she don't sing that funny old song any more
> Rook tooky tooky took took tooky took took took
> That's what she said all the while.

On our farm, hens died all the time when we needed them for a meal, so the old hen's demise didn't distress me.

The Flin Flon trip is hazy in my memory. I wasn't part of the pottery-making lessons. Mum, Lynette, and I stayed with family friends in their lovely house with running water and comfortable beds. They also had a television and Lynette and I were excited to see The Beatles on *The Ed Sullivan Show*. I remember the adult disgust at such terrible "entertainment." In fact, we watched an appearance the Fab Four had taped, after their initial live performance in February 1964, for Sullivan to broadcast later that year.

While Grandma took her pottery and ceramic lessons, Grandpa, Mum, Lynette, and I toured Flin Flon. The houses built on rock and the rustic look of the town astonished me. Accustomed to our farm, with its house situated on the flat land of the prairie, I thought climbing stairs built over a rock face to get to a house must be tiring. Imagine carrying groceries up all those stairs!

In awe of both the house we stayed in and the house where Grandma took her pottery lessons, I learned that a couch and chair could match and that all the furniture in a bedroom could be a similar design and colour.

We bought gifts to take home to Daddy and Edward, and Grandma bought supplies for her new hobby. I missed Edward and Daddy and wondered if they were okay. I ran into Daddy's arms the minute we got back to the farm and, once again, the farmhouse surrounded us. In my child's innocence, I believed our lives could not be more perfect and nothing bad could ever happen with Daddy's arms ready to envelop us.

*Made Edward a tiger costume using flannelette
with a tiger pattern... I made Rosalie a tiger
costume... The Hallowe'en party was today. Both
Edward and Rosalie got prizes for best costume—
each got a twenty-cent chocolate nut bar.*

WHILE IN Daddy's arms, I would have been looking over his shoulder for Edward. I followed Daddy around the farm like a small shadow but, whether he liked it or not, I became Edward's smaller conjoined twin. Seven years my senior, he got stuck caring for me because Lynette, the eldest, had to help hoe the garden or cook.

After school and on summer days, Edward and I could most often be found together. Generally, careful of my welfare, he placed me in cardboard boxes where he could see me and then would continue with his own projects. If he chose the back pasture as the site of his new fort, he made sure I could not be hit by falling poplar trees. I never heard any stories about my disliking this arrangement because I think I was happy just to be in his presence. With his dark blond hair and almost cherubic face inherited from Mum, Edward had our father's wild sense of humour. While he protected me, I was often the butt of his antics. His sense of what constituted a good joke became more refined as he got older, but he tested most of his gags on me first.

Edward, like all Canadian kids, had dreams of playing hockey. Each winter, he cleared a space on the frozen dugout for his imaginary games. He had no skates because our family had no money for sports equipment. When Lynette wanted to curl, my parents had to budget carefully to find the $1.50 to buy her a broom. So, Edward practised his moves with imaginary equipment. He would run a few feet and then slide on his winter boots, shouting a play-by-play as he took a pass from Henri Richard and fired a shot on Terry Sawchuk. He always scored on the imaginary net with his imaginary puck!

One day, as he practised, he urged me to try his technique and glide across the rink. Fear gripped me at the prospect.

"C'mon, Rosie, try it," he coaxed. "I'll catch you!"

After much cajoling, I made my initial run, planted my feet, and slid toward him. But, like Lucy pulling the football away from Charlie Brown in the *Peanuts* cartoon, when I neared Edward's arms, he stepped aside. I fell flat on my face. Blood gushed from my nose. My screams brought Daddy running from the barn to find my contrite brother trying to comfort me. Daddy scooped me up and ran to the house directing a dressing down at Edward, who followed. In the kitchen, Mum removed my winter clothes while Daddy returned outside to scoop up snow to pack on my face to stop the bleeding. Taking me to a hospital wasn't discussed. The car likely wouldn't have started and Rusty and Jumbo couldn't make a trip of that distance in the cold. Daddy used his army medical training to assess and treat my injury and the bleeding eventually stopped. I don't know if Mum ever got the blood stains removed from my parka. I am plagued with sinus issues and nosebleeds even now and I wonder if it can all be traced back to this prank gone horribly wrong.

Edward and I accompanied our father into the bush to gather wood for the coming winter. Rusty and Jumbo were hitched to a flatbed wagon and my brother and father sawed down trees and filled it. I had to heed their cautions to stay out of the way of falling trees. It must have been June because the army worms were munching their way through the poplar trees by the thousands. With the wagon loaded, Daddy took up the reins and told Edward to sit on the load behind me to make sure I didn't fall off. Unbeknownst to me, he amused himself by filling the hood of my jacket with army worms that he picked off the felled trees. When he couldn't find any more worms to add to the writhing collection, he slipped the hood over my head. Worms cascaded over my face and into my clothes. Again, alerted by my screams, Daddy bawled Edward out, ordering him to find and remove every worm from my person. To this day, I blame Edward for my dislike of worms!

Edward's youthful pranks at my expense in no way disrupted my worship of him. I stood ready to play Robin to his Batman or be on the losing end of a wrestling match between Bruno Sammartino and Whipper Billy Watson, whose matches Edward followed on the radio. On a whim, he would say, "You be Bruno." Then we would tussle, with him, being larger, always winning.

In an experiment, likely prompted by a physics lesson at school, he put me in our old wooden wagon and pushed me off the top of the hill of dirt created by the excavation of our basement. I hurtled down the hill across the wild grass that passed for a lawn towards the outhouse and a stand of spruce trees. I remember hanging on for dear life while he hollered from the top of the hill to not let go. We worked through that experiment several times while he tried to gauge the effort of his push to where I would finally come to a stop. Thankfully, I never got as far as the trees or the outhouse no matter how hard he pushed. If I had, it could have been a repeat of the frozen dugout incident or worse.

"What possessed you to send me hurtling down the hill in the wagon?" I once asked. "What if it had hit something?"

"I made sure you had the handle to steer," he reasoned. I often accused him of "torturing" me. In reality, the memories make me smile.

If Edward used me to test his ideas, such as putting me on a calf to see if I could accomplish an eight-second bull ride, he also took his role as protector seriously. No other kid dared pick on his little sister, which once caused an argument between Mum and a neighbour about whether Edward should have stepped in to save me from being bullied. The neighbour accused Edward of bullying when he rescued me from her son, who had pushed me to the ground. The fact her kid was larger than me didn't factor into her understanding of the incident. Despite the pranks, I knew Edward had my back, which he proved over and over.

*The doctor was having Danny moved to Dauphin. Why
Dauphin when Danny asked to go to Deer Lodge? I talked to
him, combed his hair and was doing his finger nails when
the nurses came to get him ready to move—the ambulance
had arrived. I wanted to go with him so much but Daddy
said that he was going. When I said that I wanted to go
with Danny, he said, "you have chores and the children to
take care of." After all the help that Danny gave my family,
there is no one to stay at the farm with my children. Daddy
stayed in the room and sent me to his car for his glasses,
and when I got back the nurses would not let me in the
room because two big ambulance drivers and another man
were in there and they could hardly move. They wheeled
Danny out of the room, past me and down the hall and
wouldn't stop so that I could say "good-bye." I went to
the waiting room and sat down and cried and cried.*

IN DECEMBER, a few months after the Flin Flon vacation, our lives were turned upside down. The farmhouse and my parents' plans for it could not shelter us from the emotional storm on the horizon. Within a year, a different house would shelter us.

Daddy, as usual, went to the barn after supper to do the evening chores. I don't know if he completed his work, but a little while later he came staggering to the house suffering severe abdominal pain. He said he'd lain in the straw in the barn for a while hoping it would subside, but then decided he might be better off in the house. As he lay on the bed moaning, he and Mum decided he should go to the hospital.

We still didn't have a phone, and Lynette, who had learned to drive in the summer, hadn't driven in the winter. Even if she tried to make the trip, our 1949 Oldsmobile, which replaced the 1930 Plymouth a few months after I was born, did not run well in cold weather. Its battery had a permanent resting place beside the stove! The neighbours had a phone and Edward set out for their farm to get help. He walked the quarter mile in the bitter cold and through blowing snow. My fastidious father would not go to the hospital in his barn overalls. While we waited for help to arrive, Mum got him changed into cleaner clothes. A short while later a truck pulled into the yard with Edward and the neighbour's youngest son. Our parents decided Lynette should go with Daddy to the hospital. Wracked with pain, Daddy struggled to get his outdoor clothing on. I sat on the floor at his feet while he instructed me between gasps how to put his boots on. Bundling Daddy into the truck, the trio set off in the storm towards the hospital in Swan River. When they arrived, nurses took over, rushing Daddy into the building and leaving Lynette and the neighbour to turn around and head home. With no telephone, we asked the neighbour to alert Grandpa and Grandma about our situation.

With Daddy in the hospital, my fourteen-year-old brother took over the care of the animals. Edward milked the cows and fed all the animals and then got ready to catch the school bus. Lynette kept an eye on me so Mum could take on more of the outdoor work. It didn't take long for the party line to share the news about Dan Tennison's hospitalization. Family and friends rallied to help us where they could.

I'd started school that fall and I loved it so much I never wanted to miss a minute. There is a photo of me standing in front of the house all smiles, clutching my new Black Beauty lunch box. When winter set in, Daddy had begun taking me to Craigsford in the wagon box, pulled by Rusty and Jumbo, picking up other kids along the way. With Daddy in the hospital, I started to walk the two kilometres to school. Mum told me she worried about her six-year-old walking alone in the frigid temperatures. She dressed herself warmly and walked me to the end of our road to, hopefully, connect me with other kids walking the same direction. She said she watched to make sure I turned in at the school. Looking back, I think the distraction of school helped me slough off the worried tension that filled our house.

George, the neighbour who let us haul water from his well, started dropping by in the morning to pick me up and give me a ride. His thirteen-year-old daughter, Joyce, looked out for me in the school yard and if we had to walk home. On one particularly cold day, they didn't come for me, and I insisted on walking. I tumbled through the school door to the shock of my teacher and classmates. The teacher unwrapped my frozen scarf and rubbed my nearly frozen toes. She sat me by the stove to warm up before letting me go to my desk. When George came to pick up Joyce, he couldn't believe I had walked to school. He accompanied me into the house at our farm and told my mother to never again let me walk. If they didn't come for me, then Mum had to keep me home. Mum said she had a hard time fighting my determination to get to school.

Without a phone, we got no news of Daddy's condition. Grandpa took Mum to the hospital to see her husband as often as he could, leaving Grandma at our house to be there for me if I got home before my siblings. If they beat me home, of course they would take care of me while Lynette started supper and Edward did chores, but winter travel is unpredictable and my family took no chances.

The doctor said Daddy had an ulcer and transferred him to a hospital in Dauphin 170 kilometres away instead of to the veteran's hospital in Winnipeg, where Daddy asked to be sent. Dauphin is where Daddy died—alone, with no family around him. When I am asked by doctors about my family's medical history and I tell them my father died of an ulcer, each one has replied: "No one dies of an ulcer." But my father did. Would he have survived if he had gone to Winnipeg? Could we have afforded to pay the bill for the ambulance and his care? My mother consoled herself that her husband had gone to be with

Gareth so their baby wouldn't be alone. I tell myself it was the 1960s in an isolated rural area, but I wonder how our lives would have turned out had he come home to us.

The hospital phoned my grandparents and they drove to our farm to tell Mum her husband was dead. She became a widow at forty-four. Our lives changed forever on that day, December 18, 1964. Someone—I've always thought it was George, but it might have been Uncle Billie—picked me up at school and delivered me to our house. My siblings were picked up by someone else at their school in Bowsman and brought home. When I entered the house, Mum held out her arms to me and I crawled into her lap. She rocked me in her rocking chair with tears streaming down her face. She explained that my daddy would never be coming home and that he had gone to be with Gareth. I don't remember her exact words, but I understood the catastrophic news. Daddy hadn't been in the house for many days by this point, but we thought he would recover and come home. When I'd helped him put on his boots, I didn't know that was the last time I would see him. My worshipped Daddy would never read me *Dennis the Menace* again. His hearty laugh fell silent and we faced an uncertain future.

The news travelled fast in a world with no email. Neighbours listening on the party line knew my father had died before Grandpa got to our farm to inform Mum. There's a reason for the phrase "names not released pending notification of relatives." Barely comprehending the news herself, Mum was further distressed that she would not be the person sharing this tragic information with her family and closest friends.

An expensive long-distance telephone call alerted Aunt Jean in Ontario and she made arrangements to come to her brother's funeral. The news of his illness had likely just reached her by letter, and now she learned he had died. From Sarnia, her route took her by train to Toronto, and then on her first airplane ride to Winnipeg, followed by another train ride to Swan River. Grandpa picked her up at the station in the middle of the night and brought her to their farm, where we stayed awaiting the funeral. Aunt Jean came to where I slept in the bed I shared with Mum and pulled me into in a hug. I had only seen her once before in my six years, but she never missed sending us wonderful gifts for our birthdays and at Christmas. Grandma Tennison did not make the trip from Ontario to attend her son's funeral.

Uncle Henry went to his trapline near Cranberry Portage every fall and we didn't see him again until spring. Grandpa may have written to him to tell him about Daddy's illness, but sending him a letter to tell him about Daddy's passing would take too long. To get in touch with him, Grandpa sent a notice to CBC's *Canadian Northern Messenger*, known colloquially as "Messages to the North," a radio service for isolated communities that broadcast news about births, deaths, and illness. The airwaves crackled with the news that his brother-in-law Dan had died and he should come home. So began Uncle Henry's long trek. He arranged for another trapper to care for his dogs and took his snow machine to Hemming Lake, a whistle stop on the rail line, where he could get his mail and flag down the train to catch a ride home.

Meanwhile, our house sat cold and empty. I suppose neighbours were looking after the animals or maybe my uncles were pitching in. Someone knows, but I have few memories of that time.

The arrangements for Daddy's funeral and how his body returned to us from Dauphin are also not in my memory bank. At the visitation at Paull Funeral Home in Swan River, Mum took my hand and led me to see Daddy in his coffin. She encouraged me to touch him and, when I did, his skin felt cold and had the texture of the sealing wax Mum used to cover jars of jelly. The body in the coffin looked like my daddy, but he didn't wake up when I touched him. That's when I understood I would never hear his laugh again.

The next day, in unrelenting cold, we buried my father. Small St. Paul's Anglican Church in Bowsman would not hold the anticipated crowd, and my father wasn't there to light the stove to warm the church. Expecting a large turnout for a man who represented his community in a war and pitched in to help neighbours, and whose family had farmed in the area for over forty years, Mum asked for his funeral to be moved to the Orange Hall. But the Anglican minister declined to officiate at my father's funeral if we didn't have it in the little church with its ten pews. My mother insisted for kindness's sake that the larger hall would be more appropriate during the cold weather, but the minister steadfastly refused to do the service unless we used the church. His recalcitrance hurt my mother and strained her relationship with the church and that particular minister for years to come. Thankfully, the United Church minister understood the situation and agreed to conduct my father's funeral service in the hall that also hosted wedding receptions; I don't know if we knew him.

The only part of Daddy's funeral I remember is the drive to the cemetery. The frigid cold kept the committal at the grave short while Grandma and I waited in Grandpa's car. I don't think it would have mattered if I had stood at the grave because I already understood our loss.

At some point in this period of sadness, Craigsford School held its Christmas concert. All the one-room schools held concerts every year that warmed the winter nights and ushered in the festive season. Teachers coordinated their dates to eliminate double booking, allowing people to go from school to school to see nieces, nephews, and friends' children perform. To avoid repetition, the teachers also competed to find new holiday songs or skits for their school's concert.

I don't know how they crammed so many people into the small schools for these events, but they were often standing room only. The desks were shoved against the wall and benches were put into the space in front of a makeshift stage hidden by a cotton sheet strung on a wire. Each grade contributed to the program of short skits, recitations, and songs. At the end of the performances, Santa Claus, played by a willing volunteer from another district in a homemade red suit, made an appearance. Santa handed out gifts that parents had purchased in advance for their children. Each child also received a paper bag of treats—ribbon candy and nuts.

My teacher assigned me a recitation for my first Christmas concert at Craigsford School. I worked hard on the memorization with help from my family. The assignment probably kept me occupied during Daddy's hospitalization. I no longer remember the poem, other than that it featured an angel.

When Daddy died, no one expected me to do my recitation. He had been the master of ceremonies at the Craigsford Christmas concert for many years—something the community looked forward to as much as the children's offerings. My father told jokes to fill in between the acts and his boisterous laughter kept the evening lively. The concert of 1964 would be different. I could not be dissuaded from doing my recitation at the concert. Mum said there wasn't a dry eye in the house as six-year-old me got up in my best dress and rhymed off my poem to make my daddy proud.

Danny took some snapshots of the children and the tree, and he played the Silent Night music box to wake them up, and had the house nice and warm. Sometimes I would like to have our beautiful Christmas mornings last forever...

Dad and Mother came and were here for a short while. Dad sold the belt for the grain separator (Rosalie's horsey, while Danny and I were in the field) and got thirty dollars for it.

WE DID NOT spend Christmas at our house that year because Daddy wasn't there to keep the fires going and add to the magic with special decorating touches. After lighting the fires early Christmas morning, he would always head to the barn to do the chores. With his work finished, he returned the house, plugged in the Christmas tree lights, checked the fires, and then walked through the rooms carrying a music box that played "Silent Night." At the musical cue, we could see what Santa Claus left for us under the tree and in our stockings. One Christmas, a Magnajector, a neat item that could project and enlarge images onto a wall using a lightbulb and mirrors, had a tag on it addressed to the whole family. Daddy placed it over a picture of the Nativity scene and projected it onto the wall, filling it, before getting the family up.

In 1964, our house did not have a Christmas tree. Daddy wasn't there to choose the perfect tree in our acres of bush and chop it down. Mum's few blown-glass ornaments she'd saved from her childhood all stayed in their tissue cocoons. The decorations she made by sticking seals (adhesive stamps used to decorate envelopes and packages) on cardboard, gluing tinsel around the edges, and attaching a hanging loop remained in their box. The angel wearing the crocheted dress she made did not top our tree that year.

Every Christmas Eve, Daddy positioned the spruce in a crock filled with rocks to hold it steady. To prevent any accidental tree fall, he circled the trunk with string that he tied to nails in the wall. Once Daddy put the lights on, we started hanging our precious ornaments. Besides Mum's homemade ones, we had lovely hand-blown glass birds and balls she had from her childhood. When I demanded to help decorate the tree, I could only hang Mum's cardboard ornaments. A long, skinny Santa Claus ornament made out of pipe cleaners was deemed safe for me to hang on the bottom branches of the tree as well. My siblings worried I would drop the glass ornaments and break them. We had so few decorations that losing one lovely ornament would be distressing.

One year, before Christmas, I went to town with Daddy and he took me to the local drugstore to look at the tree ornaments for purchase. On the very bottom shelf were packages of Styrofoam decorations. Each package had about eight ornaments—stars, balls, bells—and each white ornament shone with glitter in silver and gold. Daddy told me to choose the package I liked. I picked the only one that had a reindeer in it; I may have thought it looked like Rudolph. The collection cost a princely sum of twenty-five cents. When Christmas Eve arrived and we were decorating the tree, I had my own ornaments that I could hang around the bottom. Those ornaments, stored in their own special cardboard box, were always referred to as "Rosalie's ornaments" and only I could hang them on the tree. Edward would tease me by pretending to take one to hang and I would throw a fit until one of our parents would scold him for tormenting me.

The year Daddy died, my Styrofoam ornaments stayed in their box and Santa Claus had to find us at my grandparents' house. Mum assured me he would and, on Christmas morning, I saw she had been right. Under the tree, a metre-tall yellow stuffed rabbit wearing a red waistcoat had a tag around its neck with my name on it. I have no recollection if I begged Santa for it or if my parents thought I would like a large yellow rabbit, but it is the only gift I remember from that Christmas. As time goes by and years of Christmas memories collect in my mind, it is the one gift of many received that I can accurately date to the year I found it under the tree. My gift to Daddy, a door decoration with tinkling bells, sat forlornly unopened. Mum helped me wrap it in heavy holiday-themed paper that had enveloped a store purchase in the days before paper bags were common. We did the wrapping during Daddy's hospital stay to keep my spirits up. It remains unopened even now, but I know what is in the package when I find it again every year, tucked in the box that holds my ornaments. The tag says: "To Daddy From Rosalie" in my best Grade 1 printing.

We spent the holidays at Wildwood, returning to our farmhouse when we had to go back to school. It felt empty without our father's laughter. The comics were no longer read after supper and the cold settled in every corner and around our feet under the table. Mum became nervous of the house without Daddy there. He always made sure the stove pipes were clean and he knew how much wood the heater required to last the night. Afraid to put too much wood in the stoves, Mum moved us all to the living area of the house for sleeping. The frost on the window became thicker than normal because she worried about burning the house down. Until the cold weather abated, we camped in the living room using a rollaway cot and piles of quilts and blankets for sleeping. During the night, Mum would add one stick of wood at a time to the heater to keep us and the house from freezing.

Summer eventually came, but we still lived under a cloud of sadness and, for Mum, shock. Edward stepped up and did most of the work around the farmyard. Lynette pitched in around the house and took care of me, her wish come true, while our mother muddled along. In my childhood innocence, I did not know that more changes were coming in my life. My mother and siblings did their best to shield me from all the anguish, but I sensed tragedy and my subconscious reacted. I started having regular nightmares that snakes were coming for me. A radio report about a hurricane thousands of miles away terrified me. I believed our house would blow away. To her credit, Mum comforted and explained that hurricanes and snakes were uncommon in our area of the province. I eventually got over my terror of weather events, but not snakes.

Grandpa Bradley became our guardian in a way. Mum barely functioned as she faced a future on a money-losing small farm, with enduring debt and three children to raise. Her father took over and began making the decisions. In later years when she and I talked about that time, I know that little of what he did pleased her. Her grief weakened her and her powerlessness opened the door for our future to be decided for us. I adored Grandpa, but from my point of view now, I see he had very little empathy and made decisions for her without considering her ideas or desires.

Gradually, our animals were sold or relocated. Our dog had to be shot by Uncle Henry after two neighbouring dogs came into our yard and attacked him. Tippy put up a valiant fight to protect us, but he lost. Grandpa had given me two identical tabby kittens that we named Roly and Poly. I could never tell them apart. Rusty or Jumbo stepped on one, but the remaining kitten grew up to be one of my faithful animal friends. Mum said we couldn't keep the cat and Uncle Billie offered to take it to his farm. The moment the door of the vehicle opened at his new home, Roly or Poly jumped out, ran into the bush, and was never seen again. On a sunny day as I walked home from school, I saw Rusty and Jumbo being taken away in a truck. Mum hoped that I would not be a witness to two of my favourite animals being hauled away. If I ever knew where they were going, I blocked the knowledge because the thought of them going to another home or worse is unbearable.

Grandpa decided our farm had to be sold and the money used to buy us a house in town. He took Mum house hunting in Swan River. She wanted to move to Bowsman where Edward and Lynette went to school and where there were friends who would help us. But her father overruled her, saying the larger town would be better. That directive caused repercussions we recognized too late and could not correct.

In between house hunting expeditions, Mum packed. We didn't have much furniture and we probably only had about four outfits of clothing each. I mostly lived in castoffs that filtered through the family and, by the time they reached me, were faded and thin from washing. My wardrobe fit in a small box. Mum's kitchen full of baking pans and pots, our everyday dishes collected from oatmeal packages, and her partial set of Tapestry Rose fine china were carefully wrapped and put in unused wooden egg crates now that we no longer had chickens. With little money, Mum never completed her set of china, and then Paragon discontinued the pattern, removing all hope. But she used the few pieces she had for dessert on special occasions and we drank tea out of the cups, making us feel like we were sipping with royalty.

I kept Lynette company as she packed her few belongings, sniffling and wiping her nose on tissues. She tried to be brave and accept the change, but the loss of our father and now the move took its toll. She wrote a note and left it in the closet for the next person who might use her room to find. But no one ever moved into her room. The house Daddy built for Mum and our family never sheltered another living person.

Our most prized piece of furniture, the Ellington piano, a gift from Grandma Bradley, had to go with us. What remained—beds, dressers, chairs, and a table—didn't take up much room on the truck. The best chair in the house, Mum's rocking chair, with its rockers flattened from her perpetual rocking as she sang us lullabies, could not be left behind. We only had two storage items to move—a six-drawer chest Daddy made out of crates for Edward and Lynette and an antique dresser with two pulls missing.

The transition may have been easier if Mum had learned to drive because she could have gone house hunting on her own. Relying on other people to drive us restricted our family. In the summer, before our move, my siblings decided to teach her to drive and we piled into the Oldsmobile and headed for an open field. While Mum struggled to master driving, I cried in terror in the back seat. Finally, she gave up. I often wondered why she didn't take the car into the field when we were all at school, but I suspect her grief and timidity prevented her from considering such a project. Maybe she did and never told us so we couldn't be witnesses to her failure.

In her teens, Mum asked Grandpa to teach her to drive, but he said the family car was too large and she would be unable to handle it. When her younger sister learned to drive the very same car the following year, Mum didn't repeat her request. Instead, she accepted her father's pronouncement that she wasn't capable. Over the years, as I spent more time with him, I found the mixed standards Grandpa applied to women's capabilities just plain odd. He didn't believe women should smoke, but he thought they should all be capable of bringing down a deer with a gun. He didn't like to see me in shorts, even when hot pants were the fashion, but he frowned on my climbing trees in a dress. As such, I think he used his ideas of what women could or shouldn't do as an excuse to push his personal agenda when it came to the women in his family.

"Do you think you could drive the car?" Grandpa asked Lynette one day as decisions were being made about our future. Lynette didn't have her licence yet and Edward, a farm kid who had been driving since he was thirteen, was too young to apply for a licence.

"When the car won't run, Daddy put a matchstick somewhere under the hood to get it going. I don't know where Daddy put the matchstick," she replied.

Her trepidation gave Grandpa permission to sell our car for one hundred dollars. Why didn't he take it to a mechanic to have the problem fixed? Instead, he decided his and our lives would be better without the cost of gas, insurance, and repairs. Years later, I owned a Toyota with a sticky choke. When the car wouldn't start, I would hop out, lift the hood, and put a screwdriver in the choke to get air to the motor. I suspect the Oldsmobile had a similar problem. It couldn't have been too critical if a matchstick could fix it. However, Grandpa, who had repaired farm equipment all his life and could likely have diagnosed the problem, especially since the car had originally been his, sold our transportation and pocketed the money from the sale. We believe Daddy may never have paid Grandpa for the car, tacking the agreed price to a growing tally of debt he owed his in-laws for the purchase of seed and other inputs over the years. Add the farm's poorly producing rocky soil and Daddy's VLA loan to what we owed my grandparents and it's no wonder his shoulders ached from the weight of work and carrying the stress. The spiral of indebtedness likely led to the development of his ulcer. Mum gave her father a lump payment of what we owed after the sale of the farm, which included the agreed-on price for the Oldsmobile. So, it seems, Grandpa ended up getting paid twice for the car.

On an August day barely nine months after Daddy's death, the outbuildings on our farm sat empty. The majority of the contents of our house were loaded on Uncle Henry's grain truck and we left our house for the last time. According to Mum's diary, we actually moved in stages with bits and pieces being delivered or collected as time and rides permitted. But my memory is of the big grain truck loaded with stuff—the piano, our table and chairs, a bed, and stacks of boxes.

As I go through life with my central heating, multiple appliances, the computer I type on, a four-piece bathroom with plenty of hot water, a washer and dryer behind a closet door, my car warm in an enclosed garage, I find it hard to compare my present comforts with the farmhouse we lived in a few decades ago. I certainly never questioned the life we had. The house protected me from the worst of the winter winds and the lashing of summer rain, and a loving family surrounded me.

In so many ways the house characterized our family. Its mixture of finished and partially finished rooms, shabby comforts, and space earmarked for improvements that never seemed to happen matched our father's inability to get the debt controlled and our mother's struggle to make ends meet. No matter how they planned, budgeted, scraped, and dreamed, they were never able to heave a sigh and say: "Well, that's done!" If they worried or complained, they hid it from their children. We never knew how badly they might have wanted a new mattress or indoor plumbing. Daddy rationed his cigarettes and would forego buying a pack because we needed groceries. The house surrounded us, keeping us safe from the weather and the allegorical wolf at the door, but from the road it must have appeared more like a fairytale witch's house than a mythic palace. Behind its walls, my parents desired a life beyond our struggle, but their dreams never became reality.

No disaster, no bomb, tsunami, or fire, took away our house. Instead, the ending of my father's life at the age of fifty-six destroyed our lives.

Items we couldn't take to our new house in Swan River were left behind or removed by relatives for their use. Our outdated farm equipment could not be sold; no one wanted it. Agricultural museums didn't exist in the 1960s and our equipment wasn't nostalgic enough to attract collectors. In case Edward wanted to get his own farm someday, Uncle Henry hauled the equipment to our grandparents' property for storage. At fourteen, Edward could only dream of having his own farm. If he did, even in four or five years, he would not be using a horse-drawn plow or seeder! Grandpa eventually sold the belt for the threshing machine. Although happy to get the money, Mum believed she lost on the deal.

Grandma Tennison's trunks, still in storage in what remained of her former house on our property, found a new storage location at my grandparents' farm in the log cabin my mother had been born in. Mum felt an obligation to her unpleasant mother-in-law even though she hadn't visited us in years. Mum believed Daddy would expect her to look after his mother's belongings. Four years later, Aunt Jean came to visit and opened the trunks to reveal their hidden wonders. She took most of the china, glassware, and other items of value back to Ontario and we were left with the empty trunks.

Finally, with most decisions made for us, we left our home for the last time.

THE HOVEL

The only photo of the hovel, and
it only shows the front veranda.

This is our second day in Swan [River] but we are not entirely moved. My Dad, Lynette and Edward brought some of our things down—just enough to keep us going until we go back to the farm tomorrow. It is quite a change... We have a very nice home although it wasn't built around our belongings. Our farm has not been sold yet. I hope someone wants it. I don't know what we will do if it doesn't sell. Dad bought this house and as soon as the farm is sold, I will return the money he put in this house and, if I get the price I want, I will also be able to pay some of our debt to [my parents].

Unmailed letter from Naomi to sister-in-law Jean

THE THEME SONG of *The Beverly Hillbillies* television show runs through my mind when I think about our move to Swan River. My family were the Clampetts! Jed, Ellie Mae, Jethro, and Granny, heading down the streets of Beverly Hills with all their belongings tied on or hanging from the truck box toward a swanky new house in the big city, could have been us. Sadly, we hadn't struck oil.

On a late summer day in 1965, we pulled up outside our new house in Swan River in Uncle Henry's grain truck with what little furniture we had and many boxes stacked in the back. Other folks living on the street were likely peering at us from behind their curtains. We were poor people whose new neighbours included a business owner, a nurse, and a chiropractor. There may have been more families like ours, but the other houses were well-kept with lovely flower gardens and lawns; houses that didn't look ready to fall down. One other fatherless family lived on the block, but I don't know if the mother worked. She never became one of my mother's friends.

The journey from our farm to our new house in Swan River seemed like a very long trip. I don't remember ever being in Swan River before that time, but I must have been because I went to Daddy's viewing at the Paull Funeral Home down the back lane from our new house. My seven-year-old mind thought it took hours to get to Swan River from our farm. In fact, it probably only took about thirty minutes.

Today, with paved roads, bypasses, faster vehicles, and money for gas, folks in the Swan River Valley zip from town to town to get machinery parts, drop off and pick up kids at hockey practice, play in curling bonspiels, and visit friends in the hospital. But in the mid-1960s, the trip took longer and required planning. People lived in the towns where they worked. A trip to the larger centre of Swan River may have been undertaken once or twice a year and only for very important events, like a doctor's appointment or to see all the stores decorated for Christmas. At least that's how my family viewed a trip to the bigger town. Now we were going to live there in a house chosen by Grandpa.

Few houses were available in our price range because we only had what remained from the farm sale after our debt was paid. The lack of arable land on our quarter section deterred other farmers and several months passed before a buyer was found. In the end, there wasn't much money left to put towards a house for us.

Mum rejected most of the options during her house hunting trips to Swan River with Grandpa. She had a clear vision of what we needed. One house on the outskirts of town didn't get her approval because, without a car, we would have a long walk to school or to carry groceries from downtown. Years later, I got to check out that house during a high school party. My girlfriend, "Jayne," who had a car, drove us there. Knowing my mother had been encouraged to buy it, I looked around with interest. The party's host didn't have much furniture and the dozen or so people at the party stood shoulder to shoulder in the tiny living room. It was smaller than the house we eventually moved into, and I was glad Mum had rejected the tiny structure.

Larger houses that would have served us better were out of Mum's price range and, with no income, she would not be eligible for a mortgage. Mum expected to find work, but until she had a job and our farm sold, money remained tight. As I look back now, I see a lot of ways our life could have been better if Mum hadn't been so grief stricken. In her shock, she let her father, who had always been the "ruler of the roost," bully her into decisions that proved to be deplorable for our family.

Finally, as summer 1965 waned and a new school year approached, Grandpa pressured Mum to accept the next house we were to live in. In fact, he bought the house and she had to pay him back once our farm sold, which took several more months. She protested that its small size and poorly designed kitchen made it inadequate for our family. Grandpa prevailed. He believed the two-bedroom house on 6th Avenue North suited a family without a car—a half block from a grocery store, one street over from the post office, and two blocks from Main Street. Close family friends, the Garlands, were across the back lane and he knew they would help us.

Built in the 1930s, the house showed thirty years of living. The seller put lipstick on a pig, as it turned out, by painting everything white, from the light fixtures to the walls and the bathroom sink. We hadn't been in the house very long when chunks of wallpaper began to peel off the walls because the paint loosened the glue. The paint didn't adhere to the sink, either, and as long as we lived there we picked chips of paint from under our nails after a good hand washing. I killed time by scraping it off the sink with a nailfile to reduce the hazard.

Mum complained to Grandpa that four people could not live in such a small house. But Grandpa reasoned that Lynette would leave home when she finished Grade 12 that year, reducing the number of residents to three. I'm sure he thought Edward would be gone when he finished high school as well. But my brother hightailed it out of there sooner than that, leaving just Mum and I occupying the place I would eventually refer to as "The Hovel."

Oblivious to its shortcomings or the sadness of our situation, I ran through the house when we arrived, trying to guess which bedroom would be mine. But I didn't get a room of my own because there were only two bedrooms and four of us.

Mum and I shared a bed in one bedroom. We had a double metal bed with springs and a mattress. Mum tucked the flannel sheets we used year round between the thin mattress and the springs. Inevitably, the sheets came loose and I would wake up in the morning sleeping on the rough ticking of the mattress. I hated the feel of it and learned to wrap myself in the quilts or blankets so I would not touch the mattress. When I achieved my dream to attend university, I bought a fitted sheet for my residence bed!

Eighteen-year-old Lynette didn't get a room at all. A davenport left in the living room by the previous owner became her bed. She didn't bring friends home to do the things teenage girls might do—listen to records, paint their nails, pin pictures of Bobby Curtola or Elvis Presley to the walls. She had no privacy because she had no walls. If we had company who stayed late, she could not go to bed. In the summer, she moved to the enclosed front veranda and hung curtains over all the windows and across the width of the space to hide her day bed. She could not be seen by anyone entering the veranda to knock on the front door. She stayed quiet to avoid detection. As the weather got colder, Lynette moved back into the house and returned to her bed on the couch. Her bedding had to be folded up and put away every day in the base under the davenport, exposed by flipping the seat up to engage the lock that held the two halves in a right angle.

Grandpa misjudged Lynette because she didn't leave and never come back. When she finished high school, she went to teachers' college, coming home for holidays. Lynette got her teaching certificate in June and was hired to teach in Swan River. After less than a year away, she returned to our house and sleeping on the couch. Eventually, she rented an apartment with a friend and got her own room again.

Edward, the only boy, got the other room that he shared with everything we had to store. His bed was the rollaway cot that had been our spare bed in the farmhouse. Uncle Henry took the bunk beds from the farmhouse to use in his trapper's cabin. Grandma kept a bonnet chest that had belonged to Grandma Tennison. The large piece of furniture would have come in handy for storage in Edward's room, allowing us to empty many of the boxes that surrounded his cot. A tiny closet had a thirty-centimetre rod and pegs for storing his few shirts, and he draped items that couldn't be hung over the room's box collection. In hindsight, I marvel at how our relatives helped themselves to our belongings and left us wanting.

The novelty of a new house wore off quickly. I missed the animals and the freedom to run wherever I wanted. Mum walked me around our property and explained that I would be trespassing in our neighbours' yards if I left our lot. If my ball went into another yard, I had to knock on the door of the house and ask if I could retrieve it. My imaginary friends abandoned me. I did make friends, but I couldn't have sleepovers like other kids. Of course, I wasn't alone in my struggle to adjust. Mum and my siblings struggled more because they had a greater understanding of our loss.

*This was baking day. I made three
pumpkin pies and four dozen tarts for
Rs and didn't get much else done.*

---

*She had given me five dollars for supplies
and I only asked six dollars for doing
[the 25th anniversary cake].*

TWENTY-SIX YEARS after her high school graduation, Mum hoped to leverage her secretarial skills into a position that would sustain her family. But she faced unexpected challenges. First of all, in a small town in Manitoba, there weren't that many jobs for secretaries. The town's lawyers, some accountants, and the schools needed someone who knew how to type a letter. Answering the occasional advertisements in the local weekly paper and acting on tips from friends, Mum applied for the few jobs that came available. For someone so shy, I imagine Mum "didn't interview well," as we would say today. I know it took a lot of courage for her to go to the interviews, and I doubt her available wardrobe showed her to be a budding professional.

The roadblocks to Mum's employment in the 1960s would be grounds for complaint today. Even though she passed the typing and shorthand tests with flying colours, one potential employer told her she had been out of school too long. Another interviewer asked why she was job hunting when she should be home looking after her fatherless children. No one explained to her how she could look after those children with no money. She could not break into the clique of small-town professionals who hired each other's wives. When a local lawyer needed a secretary, Mum lost the job to the wife of the town's new doctor. She didn't get the secretary position at my school, losing it to the nineteen-year-old daughter of a local businessman. The poor girl couldn't type, but she still got the job over Mum. Until the advent of computers and photocopiers, teacher-generated lessons were typed by the school secretary on a stencil that was then run through a Gestetner copying machine to make enough for the class. When Lynette began teaching Grade 1, she couldn't have typing mistakes in handouts for children learning to read and spell. She started bringing her lessons and blank stencil paper home to Mum. Using Grandpa's small portable typewriter, Mum typed Lynette's handouts, doing the job for which she had been "unqualified."

Until Mum found her feet and a job, Grandpa helped her sign up for welfare. Each month, Mum and I walked to the bank and cashed the welfare cheque. With every cent of the roughly three hundred dollars accounted for, there was no point in opening a bank account. Owning the house turned out to be our salvation because it was fully purchased with the money from the farm sale. Mum's only financial obligations to The Hovel were paying the taxes and the utility bills. Keeping enough oil in the downstairs tank to run the furnace challenged us every winter, but summer gave us a reprieve from that expense.

When we got home from the bank, Mum divided the cash into envelopes—oil for the furnace, taxes, electricity bill, telephone bill, groceries. She put a percentage of the money into the fuel and tax envelopes each month with the goal that, when the taxes were due in June or we had a large fuel bill in frigid January, the money would be waiting. But emergencies happened, and she borrowed from the various envelopes to cover the cost for a new part for the furnace or to replace my slide rule when someone stole it.

Designed to provide minimum sustenance, the welfare cheque barely met that goal. In an emergency, a person could apply to the welfare office for additional financial support. In dire straits, Mum mustered up her courage and asked for help when the motor on the furnace died and needed replacing. She got turned down. The man in charge did not feel inclined to help us. Instead, we heard stories of other families being given money for a car or house repairs. It seemed like we were penalized for her ability to make do and get by with what she got.

Despite many applications and interviews, Mum couldn't find a full-time job. The rules of welfare dictated that once a person earned over a prescribed amount—in Mum's case, thirty dollars—she would be removed from the rolls. A part-time job would have put Mum over that limit, but wouldn't have been enough to sustain a family of four. She needed a full-time job and success eluded her.

Mum began picking up odd jobs wherever she could to supplement our welfare allotment. Paid in cash under the table, the work helped her buy birthday and Christmas gifts. A local doctor hired her to babysit his son, so his wife could work full-time. The doctor's wife may have been one of the women hired over my mother. Mum then made a paltry sum looking after the woman's preschooler. I became a latchkey kid, letting myself into the house after school, then waiting for one of my siblings to get home. Or I would be instructed to go to wait at the Garlands' house until Mum came for me.

Mum got a job cleaning the Anglican church that paid less than the allowable thirty dollars. Probably the church wardens knew our situation and saw it as their charitable duty to help out our poor family while getting cleaning services cheaper than the going rate. The women of the church often called on Mum to sew items for the church or to wash and iron the altar linens, which she did for free. She sewed a dozen choir surpluses on her treadle sewing machine and fashioned fake beards out of coat hangers and wool for the Christmas pageant's shepherds. I would arrive home from school to find Mum at the sewing machine making skirts for the Junior Auxiliary members. But she never received payment for any of this work. Raised to believe anything done for the glory of God did not merit compensation, she likely never asked.

In hindsight, I think these wealthy women took advantage of Mum. Maybe they believed they were keeping her busy and saving her from taking up an unsavoury lifestyle. With her doing all the sewing they wanted for the church to make it look fresh and modern, they could go to each other's houses for tea and congratulate themselves on how they were helping our poor family. Apparently it never occurred to them to offer her even a small amount of compensation from the money they raised through bake sales and bazaars.

The Anglican Church Women never shied away from asking Mum to donate food when they were called on to cater a funeral luncheon. Imagine her distress when one called and asked her to supply a pound of butter for one catering opportunity. They asked her to provide something she could not give her own family! I learned as a youngster that a good sandwich did not require two slices of buttered bread. Instead, mustard took the place of butter to hold bologna in place. When spread thin, a jar of mustard lasted a lot longer than a pound of expensive butter. On the farm, Mum churned our own butter using the cream from our cows. When the cows were gone, buying butter at the equivalent cost of two or three loaves of bread didn't fit our budget. We learned to do without butter, except at Christmas, when Mum would splurge to buy a pound to make shortbread.

If I answered the ringing telephone and recognized the voice of one of the ladies from the church, I was instinctively resentful. The voice might change, but the condescending tone didn't.

"Hello, dear, may I please speak to your mother?"

"Now what do they want," I would mutter as I handed the receiver to Mum. She would give me one of her looks that silently told me to hold my tongue. They never called to ask how she was doing or if she needed anything or if she would like to come for tea. When she hung up, she would tell me what project they hoped she would take on; she never turned them down.

Eventually, Mum began to use her stitching and baking talents to our advantage. Always the perfectionist, she made beautiful crocheted doilies. She took orders to make these fripperies that the wealthy women in town wanted but couldn't or wouldn't spend the countless hours needed to create them. They would visit Mum, go through her pattern books, and choose the most elaborate designs. After I left for school, she sat by the only window with good light in the dining room working all day to fill the order. She got five dollars per doily which included her buying the crochet cotton for seventy-five cents per ball. Now, when I see crocheted doilies in antique shops priced at two dollars, I cringe to think that

Mum's beautiful work would sell for less today than it did in the 1960s. It annoyed me then and it annoys me now that handcrafted items garner so little respect for the time and creativity that goes into their production.

An excellent baker, Mum mastered the use of the unfamiliar electric stove and began baking for women whose husbands wouldn't hire her to be their secretary. I would arrive home from school to find our only table covered with butter tarts, lemon loaves, pies, and dainties. The pay for this work wasn't much better than for the doilies because, again, Mum paid for all the supplies. Mum undercut the town's two commercial bakeries to get the work. Once her supplies were paid for, she cleared two or three dollars to put towards our groceries.

Mum developed a small business decorating wedding cakes as well. She baked the cakes and then made hand-shaped flowers—roses, forget-me-nots, leaves, daisies—to cascade over the layers. She piped icing rosettes and I had the job of putting a single silver dragée in the centre of each. She created ribbon swags and bows with expert precision. A common practice in the 1960s and '70s was to replace the top layer of the cake with Styrofoam, giving the happy couple a non-perishable souvenir of their nuptials. There are people celebrating fifty years or more of marriage who have the Styrofoam cake top created by Mum yellowing in their china cabinets. Mum charged twelve dollars for the simplest cakes and, as brides began to demand more elaborate designs based on magazine photos they showed her, she began to charge more. But she never made more than twenty-five dollars per cake.

Picking up a little cash wherever she could helped Mum get us a few extras and pay unexpectedly high fuel charges. Always a private person, her answers to questions about our family's situation were deliberately vague. "We're getting by," she replied when asked how we were settling into our new house. For her entire life, when someone asked, "How are you?" she answered, "About the same." As a child, I thought her noncommittal answers were humorous as they made little sense. I know now she preferred to keep her pain hidden, leaving her answers open to the understanding and interpretation of the questioner.

*I had apple pies started to use the
apples that Mrs. D gave me... Grandpa
gave us some corn and a piece of cabbage.*

---

*Tried to use some of the vegetables that have
been given to me, such as cucumbers and corn...
It is a beautiful fall day—oh, to be on a farm!*

THANKS TO MUM we got by, but we were always short of money despite her best efforts.

All available resources went into our well-being and no money remained for the house. From my adult view, I don't know how she managed to stay sane. I believe her life would have been sadder and bleaker without her children. She lived to support us, encouraged us in everything we wanted to try, and pushed us toward a stable, successful future. Watching Mum struggle convinced me to find a career that could not be deemed "outdated" and was portable enough to take me wherever a job presented itself. I determined that, whatever career I chose, its compensation had to support a family.

With only enough money to put food on the table and clothes, as needed, on our backs, the house became just a roof and walls. No extra money existed to do repairs or to decorate. The wallpaper that peeled, thanks to the seller's paint job, stayed peeled. When the kitchen sink became blocked and successive jugs of drain cleaner and other fixes proved useless, we no longer had a working sink in the kitchen. After that, for as long as she lived in the house, Mum filled a plastic dish pan with hot water in the bathroom then put it in the kitchen sink to do dishes. She pitched the dirty, greasy water out the back door or poured it down the bathtub drain when she finished washing our plates and cooking pots. Only the barest of essentials got paid for—replacing the water heater, new glass in a broken window punched out by the local police officer's kid when I wouldn't let him in our house, or furnace filters. Often, Mum borrowed from the grocery or taxes envelopes to pay for repairs and scrimped to replace the money the following month.

Mum's budgeting got thrown completely off kilter when a bill arrived from the town demanding payment for the sidewalk in front of our house that had been poured the year before we moved in. Apparently, all the houses on the street were to share the cost for the paving. Mum mustered her courage to ask why we had received the bill and was told, due to a mistake at the town hall, the previous owner had not been charged. Our house had fallen through a crack in the sidewalk! Someone, perhaps Grandpa, approached the previous owners, who still lived in town, about fulfilling what had been their obligation. They refused. The family had more money than us, but they wouldn't even share the bill to help us out. In today's world, a person in Mum's shoes would get a lawyer and fight the town hall. But surviving on welfare, shy, and struggling with the changes in our life left her too worn out to fight. She dutifully added more money to the tax envelope and paid off a bill that should have been paid by someone else. Looking back, I think the folks at the town hall were bullies. Faced with a mistake of their making, they pressured a single mother living on welfare to pay for it, and she did.

Luckily for us, Mum knew how to stretch a dollar. She made nutritious food out of the cheapest ingredients. She shopped sales to get ten cans of soup for one dollar. We didn't have a refrigerator, so she continued to can meat, fruit, and vegetables when she could get them cheaply or if friends or my grandparents brought us a bag of garden produce. Eventually, after my siblings left home, her two-level pressure canner collected dust because one adult and one child didn't warrant the effort to can two-quart sealers of meat and vegetables.

Thankfully, we still had family and friends who lived on farms and, occasionally, they would visit and bring us a chicken. If Mum could have figured out how to serve us the bones, she would have because every other bit of the bird became meals for us. After enjoying a roasted chicken for supper, we would get various dishes using chicken meat. When only the carcass remained, she rendered it down to broth, picked any remaining meat off the bones, and added vegetables and homemade noodles to make us a hearty soup. Most often, one chicken fed our family four meals.

Mum wasted nothing. She ate the burnt toast I refused because we couldn't afford to waste even one slice of bread. When the bread got stale, the eggs were old, and the milk had been sitting on the table for a day or two, Mum made bread pudding to save the nutrition of the ingredients. To this day, I refuse to order bread pudding in a restaurant. Mum would be hurt if she knew I refer to it as "garbage dessert."

I did a lot of the shopping, memorizing short grocery lists and paying with the exact change because she accounted for every penny. While on these errands, I amused myself by wandering the grocery aisles looking at all the cans and packages we would never buy. Occasionally, a new product would catch my eye and, when I got home with the items she had sent me to get, I would describe my find and how I'd like to try it.

Mum's response to my enthusiasm never differed: "How much is it?"

One product, Swirl Peanut Butter, had stripes of peanut butter and dark jelly that reminded me of an umbrella

I had seen at a travelling circus. Mum, like most parents, hated to deny me and it must have hurt to say no so often. But I think she saw this request as a nutritional option. Opening her purse, she counted out the coins needed to buy the wonderful product I desperately wanted to try. I hated it! The dark stripe turned out to be grape jelly and I didn't like the combination. When I wouldn't eat any more of it, she meticulously separated the two and ate the peanut butter on toast. In her mind, not liking something was not a reason for wasting it. Finally, when only the jelly remained, she used it as the centre of thimble cookies and to cement cake layers together.

For the first few years of our life in town, Mum tried to maintain a garden. But each spring, the ground needed to be tilled and we didn't have the equipment. Edward borrowed a tiller once and turned the soil for her. Mum never had the money to pay for the service herself, and her exhaustion at trying to keep going finally put paid to her attempts at a garden for a few years. When I was in high school, Mum began dating a man who tilled a garden for her and she happily planted vegetables and rows of gladioli.

The one bonus in the yard, an apple tree, kept us in fruit for months. The apples were small, but sweet. Mum made everything imaginable with the tree's bounty. She canned applesauce for the winter and we had pies, cakes, and loaves. We picked apples by the bushel and gave them to friends. After Edward left home, we sent large boxes of apples to him by bus that he shared with family friends.

Lovely with fragrant blooms in spring, the apple tree sheltered my friends and me for endless games of house. I spent many hours under it, lying on a blanket reading. Skinned knees proved our efforts to get the largest fruit from the top of the tree. I soon learned that most of the kids in the neighbourhood had not been given the speech I had about the sin of trespassing. We had no windows on the back of the house and we never knew until the next morning that someone had come in our yard and helped themselves to fruit during the night. We would find broken branches and fruit scattered on the ground in the morning.

My impoverished mother bought green chain-link fencing that Grandpa and one of my uncles stretched around the property, attaching it to posts driven in the ground. With all the picket fences in the neighbourhood, our fence must have really made us look like the hillbillies had moved in. To make matters worse, Mum couldn't afford enough chain-link to finish the job, and the fencing ran out halfway down the side of our lot. Grandpa finished the project with grey wire fencing from the farm that had surrounded the former cattle enclosure.

A wire fence is no deterrent like the pointy slats of pickets, and the apple thieves continued their work, breaking down the section of fence separating us from the back lane. It's not as though there weren't enough apples to go around. Mum happily gave anyone pails of apples if they asked. Her upset centred on people not asking. As someone who respected ownership and valued honesty, she felt violated by the audacity of strangers coming into the yard she paid taxes on, leaving destruction behind. Had they knocked on the door asking for apples, she would have gone out and helped them pick to make sure they got enough. All Mum had in her life were three children she adored and a postage stamp of land with a less than respectable house. The theft of apples was an outrage that returned every season.

*At 8:30 Aunt Margaret phoned and I could
hear dripping all the time—the roof is leaking.*

*Awoke to find it raining as hard as ever... Rained so hard
and steady that the house started to leak in the kitchen.*

ACH OF US, in our own way, struggled with our new life. Children can adapt, but Mum must have been caught in a maelstrom of sadness, anger, confusion, anxiousness, and feelings of inadequacy. We were lucky to have a roof over our heads as long as Mum could save enough money in her envelopes to keep the bills paid. Re-shingling the roof when it started to leak was out of the question and didn't happen until many years later when Lynette had enough money to pay for it. The house would never be Mum's dream home but had some features that were new to us and improved our living conditions.

We got running water! At one time, the house had three bedrooms, but when sewer and water came to town, the owners cut the third bedroom in half and installed a bathtub, sink, and toilet in the cheapest, least attractive manner. Construction stopped as soon as the taps could be turned on. The alcove-style bathtub was installed like a free-standing model, leaving its unfinished end exposed to the room. Mum hung a roller blind over the window above the tub for privacy and we used the sill to store shampoo and soap. The light for the former bedroom remained in the bathroom and the other, lightless, half of the room, now outside the bathroom, held a giant closet that took up half the remaining space. Dark, dusty, and difficult to access, the closet became the dingy hole Lynette used for storing clothing, books, and anything else she treasured.

Divided precisely down the middle, the bathroom and two bedrooms took up one half of the single storey house. The bedroom closets were so small and dark, they reminded me of Daddy's coffin. A combined living room and dining room, separated by a half wall and anchored by pillars between the two rooms, made up the other half. The shelf created by the half wall became a telephone table on one side of the room and, on the other, a catch-all for books and, eventually, a clock radio.

Finally getting a telephone with a private line may have helped Mum cope. The black rotary dial telephone became her lifeline, connecting her to friends living in or near Bowsman. Despite the miles between them, I believe Mum's friends kept her from having a breakdown as she struggled to care for her children, learn how to use an electric stove, cook and bake in a kitchen with no counter space, and try to find work in an unwelcoming town.

Mum didn't like the kitchen with its unfamiliar electric stove and a sink. Mostly a room full of doors—one opening into the living room, two leading outside, another swinging into a pantry, a fourth opening onto the stairs to the basement, and the final exposing the former third bedroom, now the bath—the kitchen's only narrow wall could accommodate a fridge, which we didn't have. Our table, wider than a fridge, extended into the doorway when placed against the wall and had to be moved into the living area. An uncovered window on the only outer wall let in bright light to illuminate all the room's shortcomings.

The pantry provided storage for all our dishes, cooking utensils, and food. Covered in old, cracked Formica with pieces missing, a tiny, narrow counter under some shelves could not be used for rolling out pastry, kneading bread, or any other kind of food preparation. Mum, still following the teachings of Adelaide Hunter Hoodless and the Women's Institute regarding food safety, declared the setup distasteful and unsanitary. The pantry counter became another shelf and Mum used our table for food preparation.

A useless cupboard wedged in a corner between the bathroom and living room accesses made no sense to anyone. Merely a large box with a door, it remained half full because it contained no shelves. Stacking items too high caused a hazard when opening the door. At the bottom of the cupboard, a huge drawer provided storage for Mum's baking pans. The "cupboard" became a space at which Mum directed her hatred of the house until she tore it out one day after I left for school. But then she had to find somewhere to put the items it had contained. Looking back, I wonder why my grandfather, or any of the other men in the family, adept at constructing wood boxes, stalls in barns, and chicken coops, couldn't have attached some shelf brackets in it. My mother, always aware of her inadequacies, likely didn't want to bother them with another request for help. While they might see the need for a shelf in the workshop to store paint cans, they likely never considered that shelves in the cavity would give her safer storage for cookbooks.

Accustomed to having Daddy build her whatever she wanted, I think Mum became demoralized by her newly identified inadequacies. Indirectly, she taught me self-sufficiency because I saw that no one else was stepping up to assist us and soon developed a "no fear" attitude when it came to banging together a shelf or mastering complex sewing or knitting patterns.

"You know, honey, you can do anything if you can read," Mum told me once.

I hear her voice in my head every time I sew a *Vogue* designer pattern or knit a sweater with a complicated cable design.

*Woke up this morning to the sound of the radio.
This is certainly a handy gadget for us. I don't
have to lay there wondering what time it is.*

MUM MAY HAVE felt relief that she no longer had to worry about a chimney fire burning down our house, but she was an innocent when it came to the hazards posed in a house with inadequate, poorly installed wiring. Luckily, none of the sparks that flew from shorting fuses or loose wires ever ignited the house. Light fixtures hung in the centre of every room, but electrical outlets were only in the kitchen and main room. Like in the set from the movie *Psycho*, the bedroom light fixtures hung by a cord with a pull chain to light the single bare bulb. We had no money to put in better fixtures.

Edward discovered a "cheater" at the local hardware store that screwed into the light socket with space for a lightbulb and two plugs. We could plug a lamp or a radio into an extension cord that draped down from the fixture. All electrical appliances plugged into the cord had to be balanced somewhere in the room and the cord became a tripping hazard during the night. Perhaps not the safest electrical set-up! Many times an extension cord—sometimes two connected—snaked across the floor of the house so someone could use the heating pad to ease sore muscles or curl hair using the only mirror in the bathroom. Our large collection of extension cords allowed Mum to plug in the kettle to make tea or powered our only lamp to illuminate homework. I grew up with the tripping or electrocution hazards, but Mum never stopped worrying about our safety and reproved me for my uncaring attitude about where I placed the cords.

After carrying the extra weight of hanging cords, the light fixture in Edward's bedroom eventually pulled loose from the ceiling connection. We tried various types of tape to join the pieces, but the tape dried out and the fixture would fall down again, secured only by its connected electrical wires. Finally, Mum, recognizing the potential fire hazard, decreed we could no longer use that fixture and the bedroom remained without light as long as the house stood. It astonishes me to this day that neither Grandpa or Uncle Henry, who did all the wiring at Wildwood, did not take on the job of installing a new light or repairing the old fixture. Perhaps Mum, embarrassed by poverty and hating the house, never asked. Maybe she did and was told, if she bought a new fixture with money she didn't have, someone would install it for her. There were times the three-bulb fixture in the main room held only one working bulb because there was no money to buy new bulbs for it. Looking back, I am unsure at whom to direct my disappointment over a light fixture that could have been easily fixed by crimping the outer ring to make it tighter but wasn't.

Pushed against a wall in Edward's bedroom, Mum's treadle sewing machine did not have a light. When she sewed in the evening or on dull days, her body cast a shadow over her work, blocking the feeble glow from the sixty-watt light bulb hanging from the ceiling. Once the light became off limits, she could only sew on cloudless days when the sun entered the north window and shone over her shoulder.

The lack of outlets became a greater challenge as we acquired more electrified items. Edward gave Mum a clock radio for Christmas after he left home. She loved it and described it as "a wonderful gift." Before his thoughtfulness, she relied on the kitchen clock with its phosphorescent hands. In the darkness of winter and afraid of oversleeping during the school year, she would tiptoe out to the kitchen to check the time two or three times as morning dawned. Edward's gift helped her relax because she wasn't waking up worrying about the time. However, without an outlet in the bedroom, the radio had to be plugged into a socket in the living room. In order to make use of the alarm function, we set the sound to the maximum so we could hear it when it came on in the morning.

Grandma Tennison died in 1971, leaving each of her grandchildren money. Mum cynically suggested she finally gave our dad, via his children, some of his army pay she'd kept. Lynette recommended I use my inheritance to buy an electric sewing machine. I joined 4-H when I turned ten and could only practice my new skills or create required projects on Mum's treadle machine. My 4-H leaders taught us on electric machines and I had a hard time keeping up. The money from Grandma Tennison bought me the electric sewing machine featured on the back of the Sears catalogue, including the cabinet to house it. I could barely contain my excitement when a cousin helped me bring it home from the Sears office in her car. However, we faced a predicament of where to put the machine in a house with few outlets.

"We better put it in the corner where the TV is," Mum decided.

"Where do we put the TV?" Our small black and white television, a gift from my siblings, currently occupied that corner on a chair.

"We'll put the TV on the leaf of the machine cabinet." Between the two of us, we moved furniture, unplugged the TV and radio that shared the outlet, and moved my machine into position, leaving room to open the leaf. I crawled under the cabinet to plug in both appliances.

"We could plug the radio into the living room outlet," I suggested. I crawled around the baseboards and moved it to the other side of the half wall. The remaining free plug-in we used for the ins and outs of the iron, hair dryer, and vacuum. The downside of the furniture shuffle was

Mum's prized clock radio could only be seen in the room it faced and we had to walk around the wall to check the time.

Every new electrical item required a discussion between Mum and me as to its placement. The kitchen outlet that supplied power to the wall clock could be accessed in the dining room with an extension cord so Mum could use her beater at the dining table/kitchen counter. In the kitchen, Mum put her bowl or kettle on a stool near the stove to make use of a single plug-in on the range. Ultimately, the position of the outlets dictated the location of any appliance.

*Got up this morning and the furnace
wasn't working. I phoned Mr B and
he came right over. I had to buy a new
motor, air filter, etc., which cost $35.50.*

---

*The biggest thing of the day is that
we got the taxes paid—151 dollars.*

---

*Got fuel yesterday—160 gal—and it cost
$37.92, the most that I have ever needed.
Hope the cold weather lets up soon.*

---

*Rosalie went to the basement and bumped
her head so hard that the tears wouldn't
stop running. I felt so sorry.*

A WIDOW WITH three children in school, a house too small for four people, no money, no job, a daughter who hoped to go to teachers' college in a year, and stacks of unpacked boxes, Mum must have been overwhelmed. Every time she came home from another failed interview, walking into the perpetually dark house had to feel like walking into the centre of a dark cloud. While Mum's friends kept her sane via phone calls, her children might have been who really saved her. Every morning, she got up, made breakfast, and sent us off to school. When I got home for lunch every day, she had a meal waiting. Did my arrival for lunch keep her from staying in bed all day or sitting by the window questioning why her life had taken such an unhappy turn? When her three children arrived home at the end of the school day, Mum provided us with supper and help with homework. She kept us clean, fed, and loved, but she must have been constantly challenged to stay positive and hide her stress.

The dark house serves as a metaphor for the light-limited life we all led. An enclosed veranda shaded large front windows and prevented light from brightening the living room. A big single window in the dining room and a narrow window in the kitchen were our only sources of natural light. Mum, who loved plants, could not keep any alive in the shadowy house. A Crown of Thorns did the best, gradually filling the window with its tiny red blooms bringing spots of colour to the gloom. The darkness did help the house stay cool most of the summer.

The windows were painted shut and we relied on three small holes at the base of the frame exposed by a hinged flap. They didn't allow for much air circulation.

Despite having a furnace, winter's cold infused the house. With no insulation and the temperature kept low to conserve fuel, the constant chill brought back memories of the farmhouse. The largest expense, oil to run the furnace, could take great chunks of our small amount of cash. A single hot air vent in each room, intended to warm the entire space, did not get much help from the weak fan on the furnace. Warm air only made it halfway across the room, leaving the corners cold. In an effort to conserve even more, Mum shut the vents in the two bedrooms and kept the doors closed to reduce the amount of space being heated. I would get up in the morning, grab my clothes, and run to the living room to dress in front of a vent. Memories of dressing in our farmhouse when I put my clothes on in front of the wood stove, or in bed under the blankets, assailed me at those times. Cold bedrooms sap my energy to this day and, until I am warm, I can't sleep.

Once my siblings no longer lived in the house, Mum and I huddled beside the two hot air furnace vents in the evening. If I had homework, I sat at the table beside the hot air register in the dining room. Mum would occupy a small hassock next to the vent in the living room. The hassock's clever design comprised six empty one-quart juice cans (probably tomato juice because our family consumed a lot of it) individually padded and placed around a seventh can. More padding and fabric covered the entire unit. I don't know who made the hassocks, but every family had one. They might have been a Christmas gift that cleverly recycled tin cans before the advent of the environmental movement. The perfect height for a small child, the drop down to the hassock became greater as I grew. Taking turns at the two vents, we stayed warm.

If we were playing Scrabble, we sat at the corner of the table closest to the vent with a pot of hot tea. If Mum needed to use the table, I sat by the living room vent reading my book. Our only furniture was Lynette's davenport and a big comfy chair across the room beside the telephone—both far from the vents. I wonder now why we didn't put a kitchen chair at the other vent and then use the hassock to raise our feet. Perhaps the ability to see the comfort in a small change was overshadowed by our perpetual struggle to stay warm.

The cellar of the house could have been the set for a horror movie. Missing was an audience screaming at the teenager, "Don't go down there!" Narrow wooden steps descended along an outside wall that oozed moisture. Two-thirds of the way down, a tiny landing turned the stairs toward the dark space below. A floor joist crossed above the landing and one had to duck in order to take the last three steps down onto the uneven cement floor. As a child, I never had to worry about ducking, but a growth spurt hammered home the hazard. As I ran downstairs to retrieve something for Mum, I thwacked my head hard on the joist as I turned on the landing to continue my descent. An excruciating headache and a large goose egg on the top of my forehead alerted me to my increasing height. Going into the basement must have been a challenge for Uncle Henry and Edward, whose heights topped out near six feet, because the ceiling height with the joists spaced overhead hovered between six and seven feet.

A single light bulb hung down from the centre of the space, but the light never reached the corners. The furnace took pride of place in the middle of the cavity and, depending on which side of it you stood on, you had either light or darkness because of the light's position. Wooden shelves around the perimeter provided storage for Mum's canned goods and anything "too good to throw away." She put a cheater outlet between the lightbulb and the socket in order to have a place to plug in her wringer washer. She did our laundry under the single lightbulb in the dank, dark cement hole, moving washing from the washer's drum through the wringer into a galvanized tub for rinsing and then back through the wringer. We hauled the damp laundry upstairs and hung it on the clothesline outside the back door. When the back porch fell off and she could no longer access the clothesline, Mum hung our laundry over chairs around the house, on an improvised line over the bathtub, and one larger line strung from shelf to shelf in the basement. This unnecessarily increased the humidity in the house year-round, even during the dry winter months because the basement seeped moisture continuously. Anything hung in the basement, such as our flannelette sheets, took days to dry and smelled musty.

In the spring, the basement partially flooded. Depending on how dry the winter had been, there could be anywhere from dampness on the floor to two inches of water. If Mum sent me downstairs to get some canned fruit or vegetables for our supper, I wore my rubber boots, aiming for the shallowest spots. After the water receded and the floor dried, I hopscotched in my hand-knit slippers from dry spot to dry spot. The uneven floor allowed some puddles to remain well into June. A heavy rainstorm during the summer replenished the puddles on the basement floor.

If the floor had water on it, Mum wouldn't do laundry for fear of electrocution while working with the electrified wringer washer. Therefore, whenever water covered the basement floor, she hand washed our clothes in the bathtub. She scrubbed her hands raw keeping our few items of clothing clean.

We lost many belongings thanks to the wet basement. When we moved into the house and ran out of storage upstairs, our cardboard boxes were put downstairs on the shelves or stacked on the floor to be dealt with later. When the basement flooded, the boxes got wet and the contents became soggy. It just added to Mum's sadness over our changed life as she threw out items she considered precious, such as her carefully preserved wedding corsage. As I began to retrace and interpret her life for this memoir, I discovered that Mum's diaries for the war years and the earliest years at the farmhouse are missing. A dedicated diarist, I suspect those years may have turned to pulp the first time we experienced The Hovel's floods.

Not helping the dampness, a large cistern took up a corner of the basement. Close to being full year-round, it caught the runoff from the rain or snow melt via the eavestrough. It proved to be a very useful mousetrap as we would skim the floating bodies off the top every time we went downstairs to get some water for watering plants or for other non-consumable uses. I don't remember having mice on the main floor of the house, but we had plenty in the basement.

Lynette developed allergies after we moved to Swan River. She blamed the dust she inhaled while sleeping on the veranda but, with today's concerns about mould in houses, I wonder if they were caused by whatever grew in the clammy basement we lived over.

While I sensed Mum's dislike of the house and the town of 2,500 during our early years of living in Swan River, the town offered many new adventures for me. I am sure Mum must have been pleased that I adapted so well, but she may also have envied my innocence. I don't think young children have the capacity to recognize the nuances of human emotions. I may have felt Mum's sadness, but I don't think I identified its source. Instead of envy, Mum may have been relieved I didn't understand.

*This afternoon, a man that had been here a few
weeks ago to see if he could cut the maple trees at the
back alley, came and asked if he could cut maple tree
branches at the front. I told him that he could and he said,
"I don't suppose the boss would be around?" I said that
I was the boss and, after a pause of surprise, he smiled.*

OUR LIVES took on a routine as we settled into our new living quarters and learned our way around town. My siblings had a tough time adjusting, I think, because they left everything and everyone they knew when we moved. As the youngest, my memories of our former life covered only a two- or three-year span. I missed our animals and the ability to run freely wherever I wanted, but I didn't have my siblings' history of friends they had gone to school with for a decade or their farm ethic, where everyone has a role to play.

Lynette got through her last year of high school and graduated with strangers. In one year, she had no time to make long-lasting friendships. Meanwhile, the friends she grew up with, and who likely knew her secrets, graduated from Bowsman High School.

Using the money paid from a small insurance policy Daddy had, she moved to Brandon to begin teacher's college. As I watched her walk to the depot, a half block from our house, and the bus that would take her away from us, I became hysterical. It must have taken all Mum's kindness and patience to convince me that my beloved sister's departure didn't suggest that she was going away to die. Lynette regularly wrote letters and came home for Christmas and Easter, convincing me that she was alive and well. My joy knew no bounds when she got her teacher's certificate and began teaching at my school. Teachers were revered in those days, and one of the eight in my school was related to me!

Edward struggled with our new situation. Mum's paranoia about how he would get on in life didn't help. Repeatedly told by well-meaning friends that "it's hard to raise a boy in town without a father," she worried constantly. Edward, outgoing and fun like Daddy, made friends easily. He desperately wanted a car, but Mum had no money to buy one, much less put gas in it and purchase insurance. Luckily, other boys had cars and they took him to the dances in the other towns, and often he would see his friends from Bowsman. But the change to his world unseated him academically and he began to struggle in school. Mum nagged and tried to help him, but her teenage son didn't want her help. She believed she let our father down by not fulfilling his dying instruction to "keep the boy in school." In that regard she failed, but she did not fail in raising a caring, hardworking young man.

Almost immediately upon moving to Swan River, Edward got jobs. Likely people knew our family needed help, but soon he had a reputation as a hard worker who always showed up. He earned pocket money shovelling sidewalks for neighbours and he began mowing lawns. He saved enough from his earnings to buy his own lawn mower. He looked after its maintenance and dragged it to the homes of all the widows in the neighbourhood, who loved and trusted him. Eventually, Edward got work at a local garage because he mowed the owner's mother's lawn. Next, he took a job at the grocery store down the street from us, stocking shelves, packing groceries, and sometimes carrying them home for the widows whose lawns he mowed and sidewalks he shovelled.

Edward's grocery store job helped our family in many ways. A friend of Uncle Henry's, the owner may have been keeping an eye on us. If packages were torn and could not be put out for sale, Edward's boss would tell him to take them home. It helped Mum to occasionally get a bag of flour or a badly dented tin of tomatoes that no one would buy or that couldn't be sold.

During one of our first winters in the house, the freezer at the grocery store broke and repairs and parts had to be sourced elsewhere, taking several days. With all the frozen food in danger of being lost, Edward offered to put it in our "freezer," the enclosed, unheated veranda. The grocery delivery van pulled up at our house and several large boxes of amazing frozen goods found a place in our veranda. The store owner, likely as a thank-you, told Edward we could eat whatever we wanted of the safely stored bounty. But Mum wouldn't let us touch a thing. I remember looking through the boxes and seeing items I couldn't believe existed—frozen cakes, tropical fruit, and Blue Boy ice cream. Edward convinced Mum we should try one of the frozen desserts because it had partially thawed during the transport to our house. When the store's freezer was repaired, the delivery truck came and took the food back to the store, where it sold for half price. Edward's ingenuity did not go unnoticed by his grateful boss, who would send him home with samples of new products. We might get an entire box of samples if the owner decided not to stock the item. Occasionally, Edward would purchase items for us to try—a different kind of cheese, kits for making pizza or spaghetti, or a new brand of chocolate syrup for flavouring milk.

Edward used his money to buy things he wanted that Mum couldn't afford. He bought his own clothes and amassed a collection of record albums and 45s. But he also helped the family. The grocery store where he worked had once been half of a general store. The main store split when two brothers took over the business from their father. The dry goods section of the former general store carried everything from clothing to fabric for my 4-H projects. One day, Edward came home from work with a package for me. Inside, I found a pair of orange Bermuda shorts, a matching white-and-orange-striped sleeveless top, orange knee highs, and a length of orange velvet ribbon to "tie up her bonny brown hair." I lived in that outfit all summer and only gave it up when the weather turned cold. By the next summer, I had outgrown it.

But we lived in a small town and it didn't take long before news of Edward's grocery store job reached the welfare office. Mum received a call telling her his wages would be deducted from our monthly cheque. To her credit, Mum stood up to the welfare agent. She explained Edward earned the money, and penalizing a teenager for trying to gain work experience flew in the face of decency. She pointed out what he made didn't come close to the amount of money she was allowed above that provided by welfare. Edward only earned seventy-five cents per hour and probably only made about five bucks a week, perhaps more if he could get a longer shift. Edward said he hated the man at the welfare office. "That guy bullied and picked on us," he told me years later when I asked him about his memories of our life in Swan River.

The summer Edward turned seventeen, he begged Mum to let him go to Thompson. Friends from our old life had given up their farm and headed north in search of something better, and the sons asked him to visit. Mum made him promise to come home in August to go back to school, but he never did. He got a good job, bought a car, and came home for occasional visits, always bringing me clothes—but I lost my protector.

Rosalie said that she had an embarrassing day. Her teacher asked her what she was doing. She said, "Reading." He said, "What page?" to which she replied, "page one." He told her that they were on page two and she told him that she was a slow reader. Then he asked her to work question six on the board and when she got up there, it had been worked. She went to her seat and the teacher said that since she was willing to do problems to do number one, which she did. She said that everyone, including the teacher, was laughing.

My SIBLINGS and I had vastly different school experiences but, in some ways, no less traumatic. My transition from a one-room country schoolhouse to a multi-classroom town school, where I entered Grade 2, terrified me. Being the new kid in a classroom, with double the number of students than my entire former school, amplified my shyness.

Until our move, Craigsford School, with its dozen or so students from Grades 1 to 8 in one room, informed my experience of how school worked. Lynette and Edward went there each day, coming home with reports of what they learned, spiced up with neighbourhood gossip heard from the other kids. Without money for entertainment, such as movies, and no television, my family read books. To amuse themselves and me, my siblings read to me as I lay in my crib. Our parents read stories aloud at night to entertain the family. I desperately wanted to read and couldn't wait to find out what else school offered.

With so many age groups in the country schools, the older kids looked after the younger ones, and I knew them all, their parents, and which farms they lived on. At recess and during lunch, all the ages played together and, in the hierarchy of ability, the youngest filled the outfield for baseball games. As we grew in size and skill, we moved up to play on the bases and the newest young ones would be relegated to the vacated positions. Two-hole boys' and girls' outhouses were where friends shared secrets, except in the winter, when trips to the bathroom were as quick as possible.

Mum couldn't prepare me for Taylor School in Swan River. The school had Grades 1 to 4, with two classes of each spread over two floors. A principal's office, a staff room, and the Grades 2, 3, and 4 classrooms filled the top floor. The Grade 1 classrooms were on the lower floor along with indoor bathrooms. A large playground in front of the school with swings, teeter-totters, and slides filled with roughly two hundred children at recesses and lunchtime. My experience of playground equipment up until that point was one swing hanging from a crossbar between two posts. Behind Taylor School, an area for group games saw us playing dodge ball and Red Rover and provided space for an annual spring field day.

Another school, Duncan, the original two-storey building for all grades in the town, shared the grounds with Taylor. Duncan had Grades 5 to 8 during my time there. The two schools were perched at the top of a hill that sloped down to a park along the Swan River. In winter, the hill filled with sliders on sheets of cardboard, toboggans, and the occasional sled. At the base of the hill, ball diamonds and soccer pitches served both schools.

Mum walked me to school on my first day and I entered a room of a seeming multitude of children all my age. Without the range in ages, it didn't take long before the herd separated into groups—the smartest, the poorest, the wealthiest. I found it hard to fit in. I had an additional condition of separateness as the only kid in the class who didn't have a father. In the spring, another girl's father died and I remember the shock of the community and her sadness. We never became friends, but I appreciated her experience, which helped me feel less like a freak. In June, the teacher asked us to make Father's Day cards. I sat unmoving in my desk. She asked why I wasn't working and I whispered to her that my daddy was gone. She must have known but she had forgotten. She suggested I make a card for my grandfather. Until his death, I never missed sending Grandpa Bradley a card on Father's Day.

At less than three blocks from my house, Taylor School offered a much shorter walk than I had undertaken to get to Craigsford. However, unaccustomed to so many houses and streets, I got confused over directions. Mum explained how to get to and from my new "city" school because she couldn't walk me there and back every day. I needed to learn to do the trip on my own. But the houses all looked the same and one day I headed down the wrong street to a house that looked like ours before Edward headed me off. Unbeknownst to me, he had walked a few extra blocks out of his way coming home from the high school every day to watch out for me. On that day, I heard him whistle. When he caught up to me, he guided me home, pointing out that our house had green trim and the one I had been heading for had red.

Knowing the colour of our house didn't help me in the dark winter. One afternoon, I invited my new friend "Kate" home from school and, by the time she needed to go home for supper, darkness shrouded the town. She begged me to walk her home. Mum said I could walk her to the corner, but I had to come right back. Later, I learned she only lived about two blocks from us in a home tucked at the bottom of the hill that sloped to the river. When we got to the corner, she begged me to walk her the rest of the way. I refused. Finally, she offered to walk me halfway back home if I would walk her to her house. I relented. When we got to her house, she told her mother she had to walk me halfway home. Her mother said "No!" and put me out the back door.

In the dark, fear and confusion set in. I began to wander and panic. Cold began seeping through my thin coat. Finally, I accidentally found Duncan School and I knew how to get home from there. I believe I ran the whole way. Meanwhile, Edward roamed the streets looking for me. My family didn't know where Kate lived, so he had no idea in which direction I might have gone. I got home before he did, but my tears of relief turned quickly to tears of contrition when I faced Mum's fear and anger. The knowledge that Edward searched for me somewhere out in the dark added to my turmoil. When he arrived home to warm up and check if I'd shown up, I faced his ire with renewed tears. Many solutions would have been better than allowing a child prone to getting lost to walk someone part way home on a dark winter's night. Of course, Mum expected me to do as I was told!

Even though we only lived two or three blocks from each other, that friendship didn't last. Kate left me behind to be part of the "in" crowd and took on the role of class tattletale. She ratted out offenders who peeked at a classmate's test answers and she tattled on the kids who talked in class—an irony because she talked the most. I could never understand how the teachers couldn't see they were taking the word of the biggest offender.

I made new connections in Grade 3. That year, Lynette came home from teachers' college to practise-teach in my classroom. I couldn't have been prouder to have her as my teacher, just like when we lived on the farm. The rest of the year went downhill from there. We had a wonderful teacher who left at Christmas when her pregnancy began to show. In those days, maternity leave meant leaving your job. Her nineteen-year-old replacement from "the south," likely Winnipeg, started her first teaching job in the unfamiliar milieu of a small town. Years later, she told me how intimidating replacing a much-loved teacher had been. To my detriment, she scrambled to find her footing and maintain order.

A boy sitting behind me took delight in torturing me. "Joe" poked me in the back of my neck with his pencil, leaving dots that Mum would wash off. He kicked the back of my seat non-stop and he pushed his books into my back. I'd finally had enough and, with the help of another girl, pushed his desk to the back of the room and into the coats hanging along the wall. The teacher sent only me to stand in the hall—the school's equivalent of standing in the corner. A miscreant never wanted to be standing outside class if the principal came out of his office at the other end of the long hall. Sauntering down the hall, he would ask why you were there. But we lived in a small town and Mum knew Joe's mother; they'd grown up in the same area of the Swan River Valley. However, she knew his aunt even better and one day she casually mentioned to the aunt what had happened. The torture ended immediately after his aunt told his mother what he had been doing.

In another banner event in Grade 3, I got head lice. My ringlets had straightened and my blond hair darkened as I got older. Mum maintained my light brown hair in a short pageboy-like cut. She would pull a section of the hair behind my bangs away from my face and secure it with a barrette. My collection of barrettes was my only fashion statement during those years of lined corduroy pants, turtlenecks, and cast-off dresses. One morning, as Mum prepared my hair for school, she saw white nits laid on nearly every hair under my barrette. In horror, she immediately called her parents for advice. The next day, Uncle Henry arrived with a can of coal oil with instructions on how to apply it to the infestation. He stayed for lunch while Mum decried my embarrassment.

"You know," my wise uncle finally said, "it's not a sin to get them; it's only a sin if you keep them."

After Uncle Henry left, I had to hang my head over the bathtub while Mum saturated my hair with coal oil. I held the position for about fifteen minutes and then endured several shampoos to remove the oil. It did the trick. The nits all died and turned brown and, any adult louse still on my head had been gassed. There may have been insecticidal shampoos back then, but coal oil saturation was a tried and true treatment in the country. The other option would have been to shave all the hair off my head, a solution most often reserved for boys. Thankfully, no one in our house smoked as I don't know what would have happened if someone had lit a match in our house that day and the fumes caught fire. For several days after my treatment, Mum pulled the dead nits off my hair, like removing beads from a piece of string. I never had another infestation. Just in case, however, Mum kept the remaining coal oil on a shelf in the cellar.

Grade 4 brought me back in contact with my former friend, Kate, the Tattletale. She and her pals sat on the other side of the classroom from me and my new friend "Callie," but she must have been watching me. The principal did double duty as the Grade 4 teacher. He often had to take a phone call in his office next to the classroom and we were expected to behave in his absence. Of course, that concept is lost on a group of nine- and ten-year-olds. I went to the front of the class to sharpen my pencil and said, "stupid math" to my friend Callie as I walked by her desk. Those two words were enough for my former friend to report me to the teacher, along with the boys who were tussling in the corner and the group of girls, including Kate herself, who were having a lengthy conversation about someone's birthday party. In the end, the only person exempted from the punishment of writing lines was, guess who? Kate. She even told on the party gossipers of which she was one! Years later, I met her mother and she wanted to hear all about my life since leaving Swan River because her daughter would be so interested. "Not likely," I thought and didn't provide her much insight to my present life. I couldn't believe this woman, who had turned a seven-year-old out into a dark, cold winter night, could be so welcoming. In truth, she didn't remember me at all.

Parent-Teachers Day! I talked to Mrs. S and Mr S. They told me that it was a credit to Rosalie to be asked to change rooms and that she was a good influence to the class.

MOVED ACROSS THE schoolyard to Duncan School when I entered Grade 5. Children in Grades 5 to 8 were considered too old for playground equipment, leaving a lot of kids with nothing to do during breaks. Recesses were spent hanging out, or we could play soccer and baseball behind the school on the flats below the hill. With no organized outdoor activities and less teacher supervision for groups of children, my school life became troublesome. An influx of kids from the other primary school in town shifted the dynamics and new social groups formed that excluded me. Former friends made new friends. Callie ended up in the other classroom and we only saw each other at recess. I made it through Grades 5 and 6 with only a smattering of attention from the kids who were discovering how their family's financial dominance in the town made them better than me.

In Grade 6, my eyesight began to fail. As a child living on welfare, I could only choose from the cheapest, outdated frames to correct my vision, as funded by the system. I arrived at school with ugly brown cat's eye plastic frames. Other kids wore glasses as well, but they had the latest styles and more attractive colours because their parents had money. I'm sure Mum wished she could have afforded an upgrade for me. Matters became worse when I broke the glasses right through the nose piece. They could not be replaced until my prescription changed, so Grandpa got out his favourite epoxy glue and put my glasses back together. Until I could replace them, I wore frames that weren't quite straight on my face because he didn't get the join aligned correctly. A big blob of yellowish glue in the centre of my nose added to my self-consciousness and gave my classmates another reason to pick on me! I remember a boy coming to school with his glasses taped together with white medical tape and the kids teasing him mercilessly. Having the attention of the cool kids redirected to someone else gave me a reprieve but I felt sorry for the new target.

Callie and another girl, "Mary," were bullied along with me. We crowded together holding hands so we couldn't be separated when the other girls cornered us in the school's vestibule. They yelled insults at us, making fun of our clothes, our hair, our shoes, our art projects. When the weather got colder and we didn't go outside as much, the teachers began to notice when a knot of girls surrounded us in the cloakroom. The three of us were in the Glee Club, and we really liked the school's wonderful music teacher. I think Callie's mother called the school and talked to Miss P, who decided to run interference for us. Callie and I had learned to knit, so Miss P asked us to teach her during our breaks. She had the best of intentions, but that only gave the other kids something else to bug us about. We were now teacher's pets.

Walking home from school could be stress inducing unless we got out of the school and on the road home before the bullies had time to get their fancy coats on. My friends and I lived in opposite areas of town, but I lived the closest. I could run home in about five minutes and gain the safety of our house if I got a head start. The other two had farther to walk and endured the taunting until the bullies turned down other streets. Callie's father drove a big fuel truck and he wasn't supposed to take passengers, but he would try to time his deliveries so that he would be driving by the school when it let out. He would scoop his daughter into the big truck and drive her safely home.

When I got to Grade 8, I thought freedom from the bullies had finally arrived. The kids who tormented me the previous year were in the other Grade 8 classroom across the hall. Imagine my horror when my two friends and I were called out of class in late September and instructed to bring our books because we were moving to the other classroom! I arrived home in tears. Mum walked to the school to speak to the principal. In their wisdom, the teachers decided to break up the group causing problems in the class and move some of them across the hall. They reasoned that moving three good friends, who were quiet, diligent students, into the disruptive mix would tone down the general atmosphere and break up the clique causing the disruption. It might have made the teachers' lives easier, but it didn't help us. I survived by keeping my head down, and the three of us stuck together like glue.

All the high schools in the Swan River Valley were being amalgamated, and construction of a new high school began at the edge of town. The teaching staff got shuffled to new assignments as the schools closed. Our new Grade 8 teacher had been the geography teacher at the high school, but she was reassigned to teach all subjects to mostly disinterested Grade 8 students. She belonged to a national geography teachers' association that initiated a contest challenging students to create mobiles highlighting the geography, both social and physical, of their respective provinces. The entries would be judged at the association's next convention.

We were probably three of the better students in the class with our homework done and in-class assignments completed. Perhaps our teacher understood the stress we experienced after the change in classrooms. Even with half the problem students moved to the other Grade 8 class, she still had what remained of the original group. One of the girls "went to stay with her aunt" for the last half of the year. At thirteen years old, most of us didn't have a clue about pregnancy. We also had a boy making his third attempt to complete Grade 8, or maybe it was his third attempt at formal schooling.

Our teacher called my friends and me into the hall. After the last time we got called out of class, we were not anxious to go. But she asked us if we would make the mobile for her to enter on behalf of our school. We agreed when she explained we were free to leave the class and work on it any time we had our work done. She may have been trying to give us a break from our difficult classroom situation. She gave us part of the cloakroom to work on our project. The room had a large flat surface built over part of the heating system, which became our workspace. We wrote to tourism offices across the province and collected brochures, souvenir items, and information about many places we had never been. We built a stunning, several-tiered mobile that ended up being a challenge to package and ship.

Sadly, Callie missed finding out that our mobile had tied for first place out of dozens of mobiles sent from across Canada. Her family moved to British Columbia the year we finished Grade 8 and I spent the summer mourning her departure. I no longer had anyone to ride bikes with and I worried about starting Grade 9 in a new school without her.

A week or two into Grade 9, Mary and I were called up on stage at a general assembly to hear our letter of commendation read to the whole school. We received a cheque made out to the school for twenty-five dollars, half the first-place prize money. Our proud teacher suggested we buy a globe for the school library with our winnings. The framed congratulatory letter found space on a wall outside the principal's office. To add to the glory of our achievement, we were told the competition had been for high school students, which we weren't. Our teacher had maintained her membership in the organization even though she no longer taught high school geography. Technically, she should not have had us enter. Mum couldn't contain her pride that her Grade 8 daughter and friends had tied for first place in a field of Grades 10 to 12 from across the country.

The move to another new school shuffled the teen dynamics again. The old high school my siblings attended became the junior high for Grades 7 to 9. One storey laid out in a square around the gymnasium, the junior high spread a bulging student body over greater square footage. Portable classrooms we called "huts" connected to the school via a covered, unheated walkway that discouraged lingering in the winter. Between running to the gym, the huts, and changing classrooms for shop and home economics, it became harder for my classmates to maintain their cliques.

I only attended the junior high for one year and I made new friends. But two of them moved away before we got to high school. Those that remained became my group and we continue to be good friends today. Grade 9 wasn't so bad.

The new Swan Valley Regional Secondary School on Highway 10 was one and a half kilometres from my house. The long walk meant I could take my lunch, giving me time for noon-hour extracurricular activities. I shortened the walk by cutting through the fair grounds and crossing the football field, but the wide-open spaces weren't pleasant in all weather. I froze my ears many times in the three winters I walked to that school. In my teenage vanity, I didn't want to wear a toque to keep my head and ears warm. I did put up the hood on my parka but it wasn't the warmest or best solution.

By the time I got to Grade 10, I knew I wanted more education beyond high school. Coming from a family that valued learning, I didn't view graduation from Grade 12 as the end of my studies. What I didn't understand, as a kid living on welfare, was how much a university degree would cost.

Being part of a much larger student body at the amalgamated high school proved less stressful and the bull's eye disappeared from my back. There may have been bullying but it wasn't directed at me, although I could still be singled out as the poor kid. Like with my mother's volunteer sewing for the church so other people's children could be in the choir or the annual Nativity play, the "in" crowd took advantage of my talents. I got a free pass to the dances if I collected tickets at the door. I never had a boyfriend, so I didn't face the inconvenience of taking tickets while my date cooled his heels in the corridor or asked other girls to dance. I decorated for the proms I never attended. Instead, I served at the prom tea for the mothers who wanted to see all the beautiful decorations on the Saturday afternoon before the prom. I don't recall resenting my lower status because it gave me peripheral access to activities that I would never attend.

Once I got to high school, I developed a "screw you" attitude thanks to my mother counselling me to ignore the bullies because they were, well, ignorant. I began making myself fashionable clothes that the rich kids couldn't buy anywhere and, if that set me apart, I didn't care. Making my own clothes gave me a sense of self. My two favourite outfits drew appraising looks from my classmates and teachers. I made some overalls in a blue chambray with a coordinating cotton shirt in a Holly Hobbie print. It was a much different look from the denim overalls the other girls were wearing. I was also partial to a two-piece fitted jacket and wide-legged pants outfit in blue brushed denim. I painted a long-stemmed rose using liquid embroidery down one leg of the pants and a matching rosebud on the yoke of the jacket. My sewing skills were good enough to get me to the finals in a provincial sewing competition, but another girl from my school was the eventual winner. The competition was open to students in the high school home ec program in the province and two of the ten finalists came from my school. It was an achievement that made our teacher very proud.

I immersed myself in many extracurricular activities, such as intramural sports, glee club, and a student newspaper, and I got occasional paying jobs serving at banquets catered by the food service students. A friend approached the hospital administrator asking her to initiate a candy striper program and I became one of the volunteers changing diapers, replenishing water, and assisting in physical therapy. I continued with 4-H, eventually getting my eight-year certificate and awards for public speaking, demonstrations, and for top achievement. While I involved myself in after-school volunteering, Mum waited for me at The Hovel, interested to hear about my day.

WILDWOOD

Wildwood as it looked
in the 1950s and 1960s.

Rosalie left for school—it seemed darker than usual, but as it got daylight, I discovered that it was snowing as usual and blowing a little, too.

GRANDPA AND GRANDMA retired from farming around 1970 and sold Wildwood to Uncle Henry to continue the family farming tradition. As part of the deal, they continued to live in the house. Without the obligation to crops or animals, my grandparents were free to travel. In particular, they liked going to Texas, where many of their friends waited out the cold Manitoba winter. But Uncle Henry and his Siberian huskies were on his trapline near Cranberry Portage from freeze-up to spring thaw. The solution? Mum and I stayed at the farm during their winter exits.

I suspect Grandpa decreed our attendance at Wildwood so they could go away. After all, Mum didn't have a job and I could easily take the bus to school. If I didn't already think of my grandparents' house as a place to call home, living there for several dark weeks during winter made it so. But being stuck at the farm created problems for Mum because she didn't drive and couldn't get to town to check on our house. The water pipes froze and the snow piled up, leaving the impression of an empty house. Keeping The Hovel functioning and looking lived-in became my responsibility during my lunch hours.

Our first farm-sitting period happened during Grade 7. My cousins, Vern and Twila, and I caught the bus in the dark at 7 AM and we didn't return until almost ten hours later in the dark. I only saw the house and yard in the daylight on the weekends. After Vern and Twila were dropped at the Bowsman elementary school, I stayed on the bus with older students heading to the high school in Swan River. After he dropped them off, the bus driver took me to Duncan School. At the end of the day, he picked me up first, reversing the process. I often had to leave class early, which I didn't mind because I could avoid the bullies.

Auntie Cassie often sent treats home with me when I got off the bus. She'd tell me in the morning, as I waited inside the warm house with Vern and Twila, to stop in before heading up the lane to Mum when we got home later that day. She sent me home with cabbage rolls, perogies, or baking. I presume Mum sent food back the other way that I would drop off in the morning, but I don't remember. It's odd they used me as a go-between when only about a quarter-mile separated them and they could have met at one house or the other for tea. Probably the cold weather and years of conditioning to get work done during short days of winter daylight kept them from wasting time on a visit.

Those winter sojourns were companionable times for Mum and me, but the isolation must have been hard for her. I went to school five days a week, and then she and I would be alone for the weekends. She rarely left the farm for the entire time my grandparents were away. If she needed to go to Swan River, to attend parent-teacher day or to get a tooth filled, Uncle Billie or a neighbour had to take her.

When it came to my task of checking on the house, Mum instructed me to lock the door once inside. She worried about people knowing I was alone in the house. In a small town, the neighbours are always watching! If the welfare cheque arrived while we were at the farm, it became my job to manage any required transactions.

"Honey, I'm giving you the cheque to cash. Can you go to the bank on your lunch hour?" Mum asked.

"Okay. Do you need anything else while I'm uptown?"

"Well, get the mail, of course." Mum would silently go through her mental list of cooking or sewing supplies we might need. "What are you wearing to school tomorrow? Do you have a safe place to put the money?"

"I'm wearing my jeans and turtleneck. I'll put the money in my parka in my locker."

Mum shook her head. "I'll give you my zippered change purse. Put the money in it and carry it in your jeans pocket. I don't want it left in your locker. Don't tell anyone where you are going at lunch and don't tell anyone you have so much money. Just say you are going to the post office to get the mail, if any of your friends ask."

When I got back to the farm that night, she divided the ten- and twenty-dollar bills between her envelopes in preparation for the next month's invoices. Sometimes she would tell me to take ten dollars from the wad and pick up bread or some other staple we needed. Breaking the larger bill would give her change in smaller denominations in case I needed to buy a spool of thread for my home economics project. She always gave me exact change, when she could, because she worried about theft or loss. If I dropped a five-dollar bill on the way to the store to purchase a fifty-cent item, an entire week's grocery money would be gone.

After picking up our mail and running errands for Mum, I spent the rest of my lunch break at The Hovel with the heat turned low to save money. I never warmed up soup on the stove and, instead, sat in our frigid house eating my cold lunch. Those lunch hours were dreary. I phoned Mum every day to assure her I had made it to school. If she got any letters in the mail, I would tell her Mary or Jesse or one of countless other friends had written. The letters I brought to her must have been bright spots in the dull winter days as she sat alone at Wildwood. Through the years, these women supported each other with pen and paper. Often they would tuck in a clipping from a magazine they thought would interest her or a cookie recipe they had tried and liked. Sometimes a bookmark would fall out of the envelope or a half dozen stamps because they knew she collected them. She reciprocated in kind knowing that even small, inexpensive items—a cross bookmark she crocheted out of leftover cotton, a packet of wildflower seeds—bring joy. She and her friends faithfully corresponded throughout their lives, a practice born of isolation and separation.

"We used to ask the postman to take letters back and forth between us," Mum told me one time. "It's how we arranged to meet or how we got news. We never put stamps on the notes because they were never taken to the post office. He just dropped them off in the mailbox when he delivered other mail."

Keeping an eye on the gauge on the oil tank fell to me as part of my in-town chores. If it got low, I arranged to have fuel delivered during my lunch hour the following day. Mum would estimate how much cash to give me to pay for the delivery based on the previous month's bill. Prices didn't fluctuate in the 1960s and 1970s, but she would add a little extra just in case and tell me to bring home something we needed if there was money left over. I don't suppose it seemed strange to the adult delivering the fuel to be met and paid by a fourteen-year-old. Most of my friends had to pitch in and run errands for their families as well. I remember visiting one friend who had to get a roast in the oven for the family dinner. Another often went to the Sears outlet to pick up the family order and take it home on the bus. In those days of cash on delivery, she likely had to pay for the parcel before receiving it.

One bitterly cold morning, the bus broke down halfway to Bowsman. We were still within sight of the last pickup and the bus driver herded about a dozen kids back to it. The mother had us sit on the floor and she served us hot chocolate. The driver used the family's phone to call the shop in Swan River to have a replacement bus sent out to get us and the broken bus towed. In the end, we likely only spent about a half day in school before bussing home again. When she learned what happened, Mum worried over our plight had we been stranded farther from a warm house in an unheated bus. Her fear wasn't unfounded as there were several long stretches of windswept farmland between pickups and cell phones were still in the realm of science fiction. She may have also had memories of Edward's trek in the snowstorm when Daddy took ill. My daily phone call at noon became even more important to Mum for the remainder of our time at Wildwood.

Our stays at the farm meant I did not see my friends. My social life revolved around Vern and Twila. I missed 4-H meetings that were held after school and my babysitting income disappeared for the weeks we were on the farm. I worried my regular clients might come to prefer my replacements and I would be out of the rotation of sitters on my return.

We were, however, included in the social life of the McKay District. After all the small school districts were amalgamated, the neighbours saved the McKay School and used it for a community centre. Grandpa and Grandma would invite Mum and me to the farm for the weekend to join the community whist drives held on

Friday or Saturday nights. Attending whist drives during our farm-sitting weeks gave Mum an opportunity to visit with friends. Knowing she didn't have a car, a neighbour would pick us up en route to the school. All ages played and the children learned the game with the help of the adults. I won a prize of a box of facial tissues for the high score for my age group at one whist drive. That win came in handy for our household!

On snowy weekends and with my homework done, my favourite spot became the woodbox beside the big wood stove. A larger, messier woodbox just inside the door of the summer kitchen held most of the wood we burned, but the smaller, tidier box beside the stove saved steps when only one stick would keep the heat even. Built into a corner created by the enclosed chimney, the box had a hinged lid on it to hide the wood. It also contained paper and cardboard to help fuel the fire. Painted pink to match my grandmother's kitchen cupboards, the woodbox perfectly fit an ardent reader like me. I curled up next to the warm stove and read the latest adventures of Nancy Drew or Robin Kane.

A voracious reader, I worked my way through Grandpa's ample collection of Zane Grey westerns and Lloyd C. Douglas's moralistic tales. I cuddled up beside the stove with books I got as gifts or the two public library books or one school library book I could borrow for two weeks at time. My library cards from that time show I darkened the door of the North-West Regional Library nearly every week and I often returned books before my two weeks expired. Besides my schoolwork, the mail, and any groceries we needed, I often carried a collection of library books back to the farm that I chose during my lunch hours. When the library first opened, it occupied an old general store only two and a half blocks from our house. But when a newly constructed single-storey library building opened a half block from The Hovel, I entered reading nirvana! Living on the farm with very little company other than Mum and, occasionally, visits to or from Vern and Twila, I turned the pages of many mysteries, novels, romances, and a decent sprinkling of classics and swashbuckling tales, such as *The Three Musketeers* and *The Scarlet Pimpernel*. Escaping into books gave me different views of the world and knowledge of how other people lived. I learned there are many ways to live a life and many places to live that were vastly different from the houses and towns I knew.

I certainly noted the contrast between the cold darkness of our house in Swan River and the warm wood-fired heat and bright light fixtures at my grandparents' house. Despite the isolation, the sight of the house glowing in the dark as I emerged from the tree-protected winter lane made me feel happy, warm, and safe.

*The snow in the yard has melted and the only
snow left is along the south woods. It was a beautiful
day. Today I watched the puppies play. They went
down to the slough and across to the woods to play
on the snow and splash through the water.*

*Teddy still not here this morning... About
ten o'clock the dog came home. He had been caught
in a trap and has a badly frozen foot. I bathed
the dog's foot and made him some warm milk and put
Aspirin in it to try to stop his crying... He certainly
begged Rosalie for attention when she got home.*

WHEN STAYING at Wildwood, my chores were few. Besides homework, I looked after Teddy, "the smartest dog" Grandpa ever had, and kept the woodbox filled. One year, Uncle Henry left two sled dog puppies for me to care for as well. I got up in the dark to feed the animals, like Daddy had done every day on our farm. Mum packed me a lunch, making sure I also ate breakfast before meeting Vern and Twila to wait for the bus. Meanwhile, Teddy kept Mum company on the long days.

A big golden mutt, Teddy ran the streets in Bowsman. To save him from a bullet, someone suggested a big strong dog like him might work on Uncle Henry's dog team. But Uncle Henry didn't want to train a mutt to work with his purebred Siberian huskies. Grandpa decided he needed a dog to replace his recently deceased canine. With the help of a young girl the dog trusted, Grandpa and Uncle Henry lured the stray into the back seat of Grandpa's car. Teddy adopted the farm and the name of his predecessor. He eventually showed genetic mettle by impregnating Uncle Henry's Siberian female when she was home from the trapline in the summer. Their progeny were Jo-Jo and Sandy, the pups I looked after.

Teddy learned many tricks besides the usual ones like shake a paw, roll over, and speak. Grandpa would tell him to bring his dish and the dog would find it in the summer kitchen or on the sidewalk outside the door then bring it to be filled with Grandpa's home-cooked dog food.

When I got home from school on those dark winter days, Teddy alerted Mum. But she would have seen the bus heading down the road and flipped the switch to turn on the pole light to bathe the big yard in a circle of welcoming brightness. After I dropped my books inside, Teddy and I trekked back and forth to the woodpile to refill the woodbox inside the door. I carried an armload and Teddy carried one stick.

Getting wood was Teddy's special talent. Grandpa would open the door and tell Teddy to get wood and the dog would run to the huge woodpile, grab a piece of firewood in his mouth, and run back to the house with it. He'd make several trips before tiring of the game. Grandpa rewarded his hard work with home-made treats and praise.

The days were long for me, but Mum's were longer. The party line prevented long visits with friends. Occasionally, Uncle Billie drove up the lane to check on her. During one winter sojourn, Teddy, her sole companion, provided an unwanted challenge for her.

An un-neutered male farm dog, Teddy tended to roam, but he always came home for supper. Then, one night, he didn't come home. Mum paced the house all evening. I went out with the flashlight to call and circle the buildings looking for him. Mum had a restless night checking the door in case he showed up. She left the yard light on all night and made several trips to the bathroom to look out the window on the off-chance he had come home.

After I left for school in the morning, Mum continued looking for the dog. About mid-morning, she found him limping home. He had been in a trap and, with his circulation cut off, his foot froze. Mum called Uncle Billie, who suggested she call the local chiropractor, a family friend. It would never occur to anyone in our family to take a farm dog to a veterinarian! The chiropractor suggested Aspirin mixed in warm milk for the pain as the foot began to thaw. Every few hours, when the Aspirin wore off, Teddy's intelligence showed. Coming to the kitchen door, Teddy would whine and Mum would ask, "Ah, Teddy, is it hurting? Do you need an Aspirin?" The clever dog thumped his tail in reply, prompting her to prepare his milk and painkiller cocktail.

When Grandpa got home, he found his beloved dog with a stinking, rotting foot. Grandpa lovingly continued the treatment, removing necrotic flesh and toe bones until Teddy's foot healed. He made the dog a plastic boot so he could go out in the snow and not get the foot wet or contaminated. Teddy lived to have many more adventures, getting around agilely on a half front paw. When the dog died, Grandpa didn't replace him because he believed he could never find another dog to equal Teddy.

In all, we spent several weeks during two or three winters and one rainy September at the farm. Family friends Gene and Susie Taubitz came from Ohio to visit my grandparents every year. Susie encouraged Grandma's interest in ceramics. She brought greenware, the fragile unfired clay pieces, to Grandma. If Grandma liked the design, she asked Susie to bring the mould the following year. For several years in the 1960s and 1970s, everyone in the family got ceramic gifts from Grandma. Most of our homes are still decorated with bunnies at Easter, quails at Thanksgiving, and Santa boots and poinsettias at Christmas. She painted ashtrays that ended up in every home even though only two of my uncles and maybe three family friends smoked. Years later, we have a legacy of ashtrays that we don't know how to display. But Grandma's favourite gift to each of us was a complete nativity set.

During that September in 1972, when Susie had arrived with the moulds, Grandpa and Grandma invited us to the farm so the three women could work on multiple nativity sets. While I rode the bus and spent the day at school, they poured greenware, painted, glazed, and, when they had enough pieces, fired them in the kiln. Over the next three years, Susie, Mum, and Grandma made at least a dozen sets. Since no child could be idle in my family, I got the evenings and weekends job of painting the cows and donkeys, which were mostly one colour and, therefore, mistake-proof. Mum did all the fine work of faces and Grandma glazed every wise man, shepherd, sheep, and camel.

The house must have been crowded that week with five adults and a child. One day when I arrived home on the bus, it had rained all day at the farm. As I turned off the road into the lane, I saw water covering what I knew would be mud. I removed my shoes and rolled up my pants and walked barefoot to the house. Mum met me with a basin and a towel to clean my feet before I entered. I took some mild ribbing about my barefoot walk, but I think Mum understood my motivation. I only had one pair of shoes and, had I ruined them in the water-logged walk, I didn't have replacements. The rain continued into the next morning, so Gene drove me down the lane and waited with me in his warm, dry station wagon until the bus arrived to take me to school.

In addition to our house/dog-sitting weeks, Mum and I spent many weekends at the farm. Most weekends involved loading the kiln on Friday night and then monitoring the firing process throughout the weekend. Mum got up early Saturday morning to plug in the kiln in the basement. We took turns during the day going down to see if the kiln had reached peak temperature by peering through a hole in the bricks at a small ceramic cone. A bent cone indicated optimum temperature had been reached and we could unplug the kiln. Then, we waited until Sunday for it to be fully cooled to see how everything turned out. With the weekend's purpose satisfied, my grandparents took us back to The Hovel.

In the evenings, as we waited for the kiln to cool, we played many games of crokinole and euchre. Grandma would read or work on quilt blocks or other creative projects while Grandpa, Mum, and I occupied ourselves in friendly competition. We played at least two games of anything with a "rubber" match, if required, on the off-chance Grandpa lost a game. When Susie and Gene visited, Gene joined the games while Susie and Grandma discussed ceramics. When a champion was declared, we all gathered around the table to have strawberries and ice cream before heading to bed.

In the spring, summer, and fall, returning to town wasn't much of a shock. In winter, leaving my grandparents' warm home to return to our cold, dark house made me sad. Mum turned the heat down when we left on Friday to save on fuel and we kept our coats on when we got back Sunday until the house warmed up.

THE HOVEL

Family photo, 1968. Naomi, seated in front, and (from left to right) Lynette, Edward, and Rosalie, standing behind.

*For a special treat, I let Rosalie buy us each
a TV dinner (one beef and one chicken) and
we shared them. She loves a TV dinner.*

---

*Made several trips to Garland's. Today we
got the little freezer moved in and that big, old
refrigerator moved out. Margaret gave me
all the food that was in [the freezer]. We
used a package of ground beef for supper.*

FINALLY GOT my own room, but I had to wait several months until Mum accepted that Edward was breaking his promise to come home and finish school. I moved into his room when I was almost twelve, started wearing some of his shirts and jackets I'd always liked, and began sleeping on the rollaway cot. The house seemed larger without my siblings in it. Edward's laughter could fill a room and his teasing kept us all on our toes. Mum and I entered a quieter, cloistered lifestyle.

With my siblings gone, I could soak in the bathtub and read my book for an hour and no one knocked on the door wanting in. We paid for water every month and Mum decreed we could have no more than two inches of water in the tub. Nevertheless, I imagined myself like the women I saw in the movies, immersed up to their necks in a bath full of foam. Despite splashing about to create more bubbles, there was still only two inches of cooling water under the froth I produced!

With no money to hire sitters and Lynette and Edward starting new lives, I became Mum's shadow until I turned twelve and could stay alone in the house. A fixture at meetings of the Swan Valley Historical Society (Mum proudly signed me up as a charter member!) and the Women's Institute, I spoke politely to the adults whose children wouldn't speak to me.

A talented photographer, Mum filled albums with snapshots taken on her box camera. One of the last purchases she and Daddy made before he died was a small 35mm camera. It may have been intended as a family gift using money they received as birthday and Christmas gifts. She likely chose a model featured in a sale flyer from one of the mail-order companies, but she took amazing photos with this most basic of cameras. She even fashioned filters out of coloured cellophane because she couldn't afford to buy the kind that would fit on her camera. She never limited herself to a single subject and, instead, took pictures of anything that interested her from old buildings to all aspects of nature. Word of her natural ability spread and she began receiving invitations to present slide shows to groups in town. She would go through her well-organized slide collection to create a custom presentation and, in the darkened room, when she couldn't see the audience, she talked about her art with humble pride. She shyly answered questions when the lights were back on and sighed with relief when that portion of the evening ended.

Once, she found herself in a conflict and could not present a promised show and attend another meeting on the same evening. In her stead, I gave her presentation. To prepare me, Mum ran through the slides with me to make sure I could accurately describe them. I don't remember the subject matter or being intimidated, but it must have been strange to have a child as presenter.

Buying film to support her hobby challenged Mum's budgeting. She discovered a company that included film developing in the price of the film and she compared the price with separate costs for film and developing. The all-inclusive purchase saved her a dollar or two. We started giving her film for Christmas, her birthday, and at Valentine's or Easter instead of chocolate. Eventually, Lynette and Edward gave her a slide projector enabling her to view her slides on our beige, wallpaper glue–speckled dining room wall. She could now see the results of her work as soon as it arrived in the mail rather than waiting to get to Wildwood to borrow Grandpa's projector or holding the slides up to the weak light at the window.

Even though our welfare allotment was reduced after my siblings left home, a can of soup or a pound of hamburger went farther. Those small savings may have helped her purchase film, but Mum also began buying us treats that she could never afford before. When I was about twelve, a Dairy Queen opened a block and a half from our house. Having a Dairy Queen within walking distance meant we could have ice cream in the summer even without a deep freeze. If she had extra money, Mum would count out enough for two small milkshakes and send me down the street with instructions to surprise her. At that time, the shop had a seemingly endless number of milkshake flavours. I could choose what I wanted and then pick a flavour for her. Over the next several summers, we worked our way through the entire milkshake menu at Dairy Queen. I think our ultimate favourites were creme de menthe and licorice.

The Garlands would invite us for tea most Sunday afternoons. When Grandpa needed to earn money to support his homestead, Mr. Garland hired him as a farm labourer and they became friends. Ila, their daughter, and Mum were childhood friends; the parents and daughter lived together. The proximity of the Garlands gave Grandpa reason to pressure Mum to buy The Hovel. He believed they would be there to help us, and they were.

They hired me to do odd jobs for them, such as raking their leaves, knowing we could use an extra fifty cents or a dollar.

An amazing cook, Mrs. Garland made apple pie or a layer cake for tea. Ila would give me money to go to Dairy Queen for a quart of vanilla soft serve. Once, when Ila was visiting at our house, she gave me money and instructed me to go buy us each a sundae. I walked the one and a half blocks back as fast as I could with three melting sundaes.

Treats from Dairy Queen were as close as we ever got to eating out. I don't remember darkening the door of local restaurants until I began babysitting and had my own money. My friends and I would go for a Coke and share an order of french fries. By the time we got to high school, we earned enough money from babysitting or other jobs to occasionally have a burger as well. But until I earned my own money, Mum and I ate at home. That may have been why restaurants made her nervous when, as adults, her children took her out to eat. Mum had little experience with ordering food and never having money meant she always ordered the cheapest item on the menu. This proved to be her undoing during one outing, when she ordered a club sandwich that arrived as a triple-decker with a huge side of fries. We laughed off her embarrassment as we tucked into our much smaller burgers and helped her eat her fries.

I know Mum treated us to ice cream or milkshakes for another reason. She hoped I would get some calcium along with the sugar and flavouring. I refused to drink milk when we moved to town because we no longer had cows and a supply of skim, unpasteurized milk. The homogenized milk we brought home from the store in a waxed carton tasted sour to me and still does. With no refrigerator, keeping milk beyond a day became risky, especially in the summer. Mum would go to the store in the morning, pick up milk, and make soup for lunch. We ate a lot of Campbell's tomato soup because Mum knew I liked it and I would get the calcium she worried I was missing. A quart of fresh milk allowed her to have some in her tea. She used a powdered milk substitute in her tea most of the time or, as we called it, dry cow. With any remaining milk, we would have rice pudding or bread pudding for dessert at supper or she would make a dish that required milk, such as baked macaroni and cheese. In the winter, she could put the milk between the house door and the storm door where it would stay cold, but sometimes froze. Once the milk became part of a soup or casserole, she would store the food in the oven to keep the flies and dust off it. The next day, we ate the leftovers. I wonder how many times, when I had tomato soup two days in a row, Mum didn't eat so I could have the second half of the can the next day. She often talked to me while I ate to hear about what I had done in school that morning and maybe she didn't join me for lunch. Kids don't notice if their parent isn't eating. I have friends who can't imagine eating anything the second day if it hasn't been refrigerated, but I just shrug and reply, "I grew up eating unrefrigerated Miracle Whip and I'm still here, so I don't think one day out of a fridge is going to kill me."

We did get a refrigerator when I was eleven or twelve. A well-meaning uncle bought one at an auction sale for us knowing we didn't have one. He arranged for the monster, probably left over from the 1940s, to be put in our kitchen and proudly plugged it in. I don't know what he paid for it, but it likely went cheap as items at household auction sales usually do. Most people would buy a newer fridge rather than replace their old unit with one equally as old or older bought at an auction. At first, we were thrilled—ice cream in the freezer, milk kept for several days without spoiling, and meat that didn't have to be cooked the same day of purchase. However, it had a problem that Uncle Henry identified as leaking Freon. Everything that came out of the fridge tasted like it had been doused in gasoline. Mum didn't want to use the milk that became tainted after a day of refrigeration. Even after cooking, the meat had a faintly metallic taste. Uncle Henry's pronouncement sealed the deal and Mum unplugged the huge appliance and we were back to storing food in the oven, between the doors, or eating it as soon as it arrived from the store.

Mr. Garland died shortly after I started high school and his widow and Ila moved to Ontario to be closer to other family members. Mum hated to lose her friends, but we benefited by taking items they couldn't move. Mrs. Garland offered to sell us their small chest freezer for fifty dollars. Mum and I discussed the merits of having a freezer and she came up with the cash. In reality, I think offering to sell us the appliance helped Mum maintain some pride because the family gave us the contents of the freezer for no charge. They probably gave us the equivalent of the asking price in food. The little unit fit tidily into the kitchen in the space formerly taken up by the useless cupboard. Having a freezer made our lives a little easier. Mum could purchase two or three packages of hamburger on a good sale, freezing some to use later. We also could buy a package of hot dogs and only eat one or two rather than gorging ourselves on hot dogs for two or three days to prevent waste.

We had ice cream all year round thanks to that little freezer! A dairy beside the railroad tracks about three blocks from our house sold milk, butter, and ice cream to the public. Mum would send me with enough money to buy a two-gallon container of whatever flavour of ice cream I wanted. I developed a taste for lime sherbet and often bought that instead. Somehow I would manage to lug the heavy container home. A square ledge in the freezer created by the compressor enclosure within the footprint of the unit fit the ice cream container nicely. We could open the freezer and scoop out what we wanted without having to remove the container.

Mum froze vegetables, fruit, and meat we were given. I don't know what we did without to enable the purchase of the freezer, but that little unit paid for itself over many years. It served Mum until she had to move out of the house.

Rosalie got home from school and we went to the bank and then to the Co-op. She needed jeans and they were so expensive that we went back to the Saan Store and got a pair for $3.99. Collected a few groceries and came home.

L.M. phoned for Rosalie to go babysitting. She was gone two hours and made $1.00—every little bit helps.

MUM WASN'T SHY about pointing out the house's failings, but she did a reasonably good job of not articulating her own personal stress. Instead, it manifested itself in non-verbal ways. Not long after our move to town, she developed eczema on her elbows and eyelids. She took to wearing long-sleeved tops or sweaters to hide the unsightly red, flaking patches on her arms. She could do nothing to hide what the stress-induced condition did to her lovely eyes. She never complained and tried every home remedy she learned about to reduce the redness, the itch, and the size of the patch. Lack of work, lack of money, lack of a decent home, and loss of her husband took a toll on her, but she rarely shared her worries with us.

It took me years to understand that what seemed like quirky behaviour on Mum's part was really designed to conserve what little funds we had. Perhaps the most personal example of this is a house of women needing feminine hygiene products. When Daddy died, Mum went into shock with the full extent of her suffering only recognized later. Too young to be entering menopause, her period stopped for months, and then returned sporadically, often catching her unprepared.

We were visiting the Garlands one Sunday afternoon and Mum asked to use the bathroom. Located at the top of the most amazing staircase—it climbed about eight steps, turned on a small landing, and ascended another ten or so steps to a second tinier landing and then turned again for another four steps to the upstairs hall—the bathroom epitomized privacy. I loved the staircase and, when Mum called me to come upstairs to her, I happily scampered up to see what she wanted. She asked me to go back downstairs and request that Ila come up to talk to her. I learned later that Mum's period had started and, caught unawares, she needed to ask Ila for a pad. It sounds like a crazy chain of events to get help, but Mum would have considered it rude to yell down the stairs and demand our hostess ascend to her aid. But calling her child and telling the child to whisper the request in the hostess's ear made the whole process more polite, to her mind.

When I reached puberty, we went to White's Drugstore, where she selected a box of Kotex and a garter belt for me then took me to the counter to pay. As we left the store, she explained that when I needed to shop for feminine products, I must wait until there was a lady at the counter and then go up to pay. This process would save me the embarrassment of doing the transaction with a man. As a teenager in the 1970s, it didn't take me long to figure out that men knew the intended use of my purchases. I quit skulking around the store waiting for a woman to go behind the counter.

Meanwhile, Mum never used pads. She had, but with the stoppage of her period, she likely passed them to Lynette. I asked her once about tampons and she said she had never liked them, but I could try them if I had the money to buy them. She willingly bought boxes of pads for me because they were cheaper. When Mum's period began to happen again unexpectedly and irregularly, she resorted to old-fashioned cotton rags that she pinned in her underwear and then washed and bleached for reuse. She never hung the rags on the outdoor line or over the single towel rack in the bathroom. Instead, she fashioned a rail with a yardstick balanced between two boxes near the closed hot air register in her bedroom. When her period stopped completely, Mum burned the rags in the backyard burn barrel.

Mum worked hard to build self-confidence in me; she didn't want me to suffer her insecurities. I am sure the community knew our circumstances; it had to be obvious to anyone who cared to look. Wearing castoffs is a good way to save, and most of my wardrobe arrived through a line of older cousins and Lynette. I wore dresses all summer, but by the time I received the empire waist, puff-sleeve, tied-in-the-back garments, they were getting thin and faded. No wonder I loved the orange outfit from Edward!

One particular dress is seared in my memory. During a game of catch, the ball a neighbour boy and I were tossing back and forth went over another neighbour's picket fence. Too afraid and shy to enter through the gate and knock on the door of the older couple who lived in the beautiful white house with the immaculate lawn and garden, as I had been taught, I decided to sneak over their picket fence. Why me and not the boy? I don't remember. I was taller and that might have been the deciding factor. From our yard, the cross bars provided footholds for climbing. I jumped into the other yard, tossed the ball back, and then had to figure out how to get back over the fence. I managed to get my feet between the slats to lift myself up but, when I jumped down into my yard, the skirt of my dress billowed over the pickets. I tore two perfectly spaced tears from the top of the skirt all the way to the hem. In my defence, I think the dress had seen better days. What had once been a lovely deep pink had faded to a dusty rose with emphasis on "dusty," and its thinness made it an easy target for the sharp pickets. Now my problem worsened. Not only did I have to show Mum that I had reduced my wardrobe options, but I had to tell her how I did it. I hope she was more angry with me for entering someone else's yard without an invitation than the fact that my younger cousin Twila would not have access to the dress in a future clothing swap.

Each August, until I got to Grade 6, Mum gave me one of the mail-order catalogues (most likely the Army & Navy Surplus, a cheaper option than Sears or Eaton's) and instructed me to pick my clothes for school. With winter in mind, she would show me a page with items for my size and I could pick two pairs of lined corduroy pants and two shirts. My contribution to the decision involved which colours I preferred. One year, I chose navy and burgundy pants with side zippers and one white turtleneck and one light blue turtleneck. Mum allowed me to put away my hand-me-down dresses when the weather got colder and I switched to the lined pants and turtlenecks. I had a routine. On Monday, I would wear the white turtleneck with the burgundy pants; on Tuesday, the light blue shirt with the navy pants; on Wednesday, I would sport the white turtleneck with the navy pants; and on Thursday, the light blue turtleneck would be paired with the burgundy pants. On Friday, I would wear the least dirty shirt with the least dirty pants because we played outside at every recess.

Shortly after we moved into town, workers began to prepare our gravel street for paving. Construction continued from one year to the next and the spring melt caused a quagmire of sticky yellow clay to develop. Crossing the street meant slogging through a street-wide expanse of muck. I had one pair of Oxford-style shoes that Mum bought in the fall in the size she thought I would need the following spring. She stuffed the toes of the too-large shoes with toilet paper, reducing the wad as my feet grew. For winter and wet weather, I wore rubber boots that were bigger than the shoes so the latter could fit in them. The boots helped get me across the mud-filled street.

One lovely spring day, on my way home for lunch, my feet sank into the muck as I waited to cross the street a half block from my house. When the crossing guard indicated we could safely cross the street, I couldn't move because the sucking clay held me fast. Eventually I lost my balance and fell into the mire while the other kids laughed. I righted myself by pulling my feet out of my boots and I walked home in my sock feet, covered in thick yellow clay. Horrified when she saw me, Mum made me strip down inside the door and then rushed me into the bathtub. The state of my library book worried me more than the demoralizing experience. Dropped when I fell, the book was covered in clay. Mum tried to clean it up but, like the light blue turtleneck I wore that day, the book sported permanent yellow stains. She worried we would have to pay for the ruined book, meaning a raid of her envelopes for the unbudgeted expense. I have no recollection if we paid to replace the book. For the rest of the year, I wore the blue turtleneck with its creeping yellow stain up the back.

My wardrobe improved slightly after Edward moved to Thompson because he never came home without a new outfit for me. He bought me my first pair of blue jeans! When blue jeans became a fashion item in the late-1960s, Mum would not buy me a pair. In her world, keeping me looking respectable did not involve my wearing "barn clothes." But Edward arrived home with blue jeans and, when Mum protested, he said, "She has to wear what the other kids are wearing." After that, I got a pair of jeans each year for school, usually something off a sale rack. Back then, however, name brands weren't a big issue, so as long as I wore denim, I fit in—somewhat.

Growing up during the Depression prepared Mum for the life we had to live. Home sewing saved money and provided variety in my faded or purchased-on-sale wardrobe. But, until I mastered the skill, I made many mistakes. If I discovered I'd messed up, I'd ball the whole piece up and toss it onto the corner of the machine table in frustration. After I left for school the next day, my patient mother would rip out my incorrect seam slowly so the thread would not break. She wound the salvaged thread on an empty spool to use for applique or hand-pieced quilt blocks. Over the years, Mum likely recovered 50 percent of the thread by carefully ripping out my errors. She truly lived by the motto "A penny saved is a penny earned."

Mum's frugality did not take a backseat to her creativity. Whatever small fragment of anything she saved became something amazing. The tiniest scrap left over from my cutting out a blouse would become an arm on a Sunbonnet Sue quilt block. She made granny square afghans using the smallest bits of yarn leftover from a sweater she or I knit. I gave her new bright colours of yarn for Easter, winding it to look like eggs. She used the colours carefully until so little remained that it could only be used for a centre.

Until I started junior high, I came home for lunch every day. Occasionally, I could take a lunch to school for a Halloween party or a field day. I, one of the poorest kids in the class, likely had the most attractive lunches. Mum would make me peanut butter sandwiches using cookie cutters to cut them into fun shapes. I would get hearts for Valentine's Day and ghosts for Halloween. She made me fancy sandwiches—ribbon, pinwheel, checkerboard. Even if my sandwiches couldn't compete with the other kids' high-class ham or salmon sandwiches, they were attractive. She made sugar cookies, tinting portions of dough in different colours then cutting them into holiday icons—Santa Claus, pumpkins, stars—to match the occasion. Using small cutters from our toy baking set, she cut animals and flowers out of the centres of round cookies and replaced them with the same shape taken from a cookie of a different colour.

Mum never missed a chance to make me feel special using her shoestring-budget creatively to shield me from our poverty.

I was awakened by the phone—the piano tuner.
I said that he should come in an hours, time.
It just gave me time to get dressed and my bed and
clothing put away. I made dinner for him and shortly
after dinner he had it finished. It only cost $16.00—
he said that he wanted to do something for
Rosalie and me because we had known sorrow.

The three pieces of dry cleaning nearly floored me. I paid $2.50 to have a ten-year-old coat cleaned. In all it came to $8.88.

L IKE MOST CHILDREN, I did not understand the concept of poverty. We just lived the life we had. Looking back, I hurt for what must have been Mum's constant worry. I know I never went hungry and my clothes, while few, were tidy and clean. If I needed patches on a pair of pants, Mum made sure those patches were pretty. It helped that I grew up in the latter half of the 1960s and into the 1970s when patches were used to decorate everything from jeans to curtains.

Perhaps not oblivious to our financial situation, I think I blithely ignored it. I watched Mum calculate to the penny how much it would cost to buy bread and milk before she sent me to the store. Those were the days when prices didn't change daily. A loaf of bread baked locally cost twenty-five cents for several years. When we started paying sales tax, she added the tax to the cost of the item and sent me off with the exact change. I don't remember being sent to the store very often with large denomination bills. I didn't understand how critical her calculations were until I humiliated myself at the checkout.

Mum had sent me to the Co-op store to buy a bone china cup and saucer she wanted to give a friend. She told me to pick one I liked and bring it home for her to wrap. She carefully counted out about two dollars plus tax in change and sent me on my errand.

Walking through the grocery section on my way to the china department, I spied the potato chips. A small bag cost ten cents, which, to a kid, didn't seem like a lot to spend. I picked up a bag and the prettiest cup and saucer and went to pay. What happened next gave me a full-on lesson in embarrassment. I walked home slowly knowing I had a confession to make.

"Mum, I did something wrong," I admitted when I got in the door.

"What did you do?" Mum had a worried expression on her face. She likely thought I had done something really bad, like shoplifting.

"I picked up a bag of chips and the cup and saucer and, when I got to the till, the clerk said I was short ten cents."

"Then, what?" Mum always waited for the full story before passing judgement.

"I told the lady I couldn't have the chips and she took them off the bill. I was so embarrassed. There were people in line behind me."

"Honey, when I send you to the store, I give you the exact change. If you want a bag of chips, you have to ask and, if I have any extra money, I will give it to you." Mum's reproach was gentle, but I felt terrible that somehow I had disappointed her. Instinctively, I knew she had many worries. I didn't like adding to them.

In 1970, the Manitoba education department arranged for five-day exchanges between Grade 6 classes across the province, with the host schools showing their area to the visitors. The trips were expenses paid, but each participant needed to have their own spending money. My family had a trip planned with Edward. He wanted to do something with us before getting married later that summer. I thought our family trip conflicted with the educational exchange and I wanted to be with my family rather than with kids who picked on me. Without discussing it with Mum, I told the teacher I couldn't go. He took me aside and asked me if money was the reason I wasn't going. Shocked and embarrassed, I explained that I would rather go on a trip my brother had planned for our family. I don't know if the teacher called Mum or if I told her about the conversation, but I ended up going on both trips. Naturally, our family trip had been scheduled for after school finished for the year.

We had two trips for me and one for Mum planned, but no suitcases. Mum dipped into her envelopes and ordered us each a cheap small suitcase from one of the mail-order catalogues. She also had to come up with the twenty dollars of spending money the trip organizers suggested each participant bring. Some of my classmates took two or three times the suggested amount and several ran out of money midweek. Meanwhile, I returned home with change after buying a gift for Mum and snacks when my hosts took me to a local drive-in one evening.

Oddly, my greatest lesson in managing our economic situation involved music. Mum didn't miss any chance to teach a life lesson and she was presented with one when I wanted to play the glockenspiel.

Musically talented Grandma Bradley gave all her grandchildren piano lessons, but only I caught her music bug. When we moved to town, the Ellington piano fit perfectly under a stained-glass window deliberately placed high on the wall to accommodate the pianos many families owned in the first half of the twentieth century. We now lived too far away for Grandma to continue my lessons, so she found me a piano teacher in Swan River. Mrs. Scott charged two dollars for a half-hour lesson. I don't know when Grandma stopped funding my music scholarship because Mum never told me until after I decided to quit. Instead, when her mother withdrew her financial support, she figured out how to come up with the eight dollars per month to keep me going. Mum wanted me to continue as long as I practised and showed interest. I wonder if I would have stopped taking lessons if I had known Grandma no longer paid for them.

We got a bit of a break from Mrs. Scott for a few years. She didn't raise my fee in exchange for moving my lesson to the Friday slot after her weekly hair appointment. She left her apartment unlocked and I let myself in and practised until she returned. She wanted someone she could trust in her home until she arrived. If she happened to be a few minutes late, my lesson was shortened so the next student's lesson could start on time.

One year, Mrs. Scott decided to hold a piano recital and Edward came through for me again, sending me a new dress. Despite looking my best, I had terrible stage fright when I saw the huge crowd in the local legion hall. I barely got through my piece before fleeing from the stage. That experience showed me I would never be a concert pianist, but that didn't mean I couldn't be a member of the band.

Swan Valley Regional Secondary School had a marching band and I loved everything about it—the uniforms, the choreography, the different instruments. I desperately wanted to play the lone glockenspiel because I didn't want to be one of six trumpets or four clarinets. I begged Mum for permission to join the band. She went to the information meeting and learned the lessons and instrument rental would cost about eighty dollars per month.

Returning home, Mum sat me down, explained how much my being part of the band would cost us, and reminded me that I already struggled to practise piano. Then she pointed out how much I enjoyed 4-H, which I had begged to join five years earlier, and how it cost very little because the organization had no membership fees. We only had to pay for the matching outfits members wore any time we appeared as a club, such as at our achievement nights and in the 4-H parade held in conjunction with the local fair. I mined Mum's boxes of fabric—flour sacks she collected and pieces of cotton my great-aunts sent to her from the clothing factories in Pennsylvania—to produce the annual projects we undertook. Each year's project—an apron, a skirt, or a dress—built on the sewing skills learned the previous year. I supplemented my wardrobe with my 4-H projects, reducing my need for more expensive store-bought clothing.

As the band versus 4-H discussion unfolded, Mum cleverly steered me toward the more affordable option. Pointing out it would be hard for me to honour commitments to both endeavours, she clinched her argument by explaining we couldn't afford both. She said she would honour my decision and, if I chose to be in the band, she would do her best to pay for it. I chose 4-H and my imagined musical career ended. At the age of fifteen, I began to fully understand our financial situation. Without a doubt, the cost for monthly band lessons and practice would result in another envelope in Mum's purse, whereas 4-H required only one or two smaller outlays of cash per year.

Apparently, I absorbed Mum's frugality and learned that it never hurts to have a little cash left over in case of emergency. Through the years, even when I barely had money in my bank account, I have had a few dollars in reserve in my wallet. That stash has come in handy when a tow truck driver wouldn't take a credit card or I have had to take a cab home from a party when my ride wasn't ready to leave.

Rosalie said that the house was surely cold this morning and sure as anything, the furnace had stopped running. Phoned Mr B and he didn't get here until three o'clock or later. My hands were cold. I broke fingernails cleaning and wore my slacks and a coat all of the time. It was apparently the fuel pump. I will soon know all the parts of the furnace!

FB called in with my bill—new fuel pump and services—$22.00. I didn't pay it but will take care of that shortly.

Got groceries at Cox's and gave in $1.28 worth of coupons.

MUM MUDDLED along putting one foot in front of the other, focussing on pushing her children out of poverty. Looking back, I recognize her sadness and feel badly that it kept her from the joy sprucing up a new home might have given her. The barest of shelters, the house deteriorated over time and she lacked the energy to reverse the decline. Mum removed the peeling wallpaper and we were left with the beige colour underneath, original to the house. Several doors and the big curtainless window in the dining area took up space, so buying paint to add colour to the narrow bits of wall may have seemed pointless. The Hovel's darkness would have made bright yellow look tarnished and dull. I innocently accepted our life and never asked why we didn't paint or why, when we both sewed, we didn't make some pretty curtains.

Mum clipped coupons to save money on groceries and saved "proof of purchase" box tops. Six box tops from laundry detergent could get her a free towel and four soup can labels might provide us with a new ladle. Mum tore the tops off the box even if it still had soap in it. She and her friends purchased the same laundry soap, cereal, or soup and then traded the box tops or labels so each could get what they wanted quicker or before the offer ran out. Some of Mum's friends outfitted their bathrooms with sets of towels collected in this manner. In our situation, we likely benefited most. Mum's wonderful friends bought items they might not normally use to help us get the number of labels required for a new towel or a recipe book.

More exciting for me was the reward for collecting Reddi-wip tabs. In exchange for several plastic tabs, plus a fee for postage, the company offered a doll dressed to represent a country. We could only have Reddi-wip—a time-saving alternative to whipping our own cream—in the winter when we could store it between the storm and inside doors. In the summer, we had to use it up in one day. The tab sealed the lid on the spray can and, once broken off, nitrous oxide in the can propelled the cream onto the pie via a spigot.

Mum's friends helped her to collect enough tabs to get me twelve dolls. We researched names common to the country the doll represented and gave each what we thought was a fitting moniker. Colleen, from Ireland, had green shamrocks decorating her long skirt. I favoured her over Gretchen from Holland and Elizabeth from England.

Knowing how I loved to get mail, Mum quietly ordered the dolls to surprise me, keeping track of those I had to avoid duplication. I fetched the mail every day and I recognized the shape of the box, knowing what it contained when one arrived. I couldn't wait to see which country the doll represented. I stored my collection in a large shoe box under my bed because there was no place in the house to display it. When a new doll arrived, Mum and I arranged my collection on the davenport, added the latest one, admired them, and then packed them away again.

My passion for getting mail started when we lived on the farm and collected our mail from Box 29 at the Bowsman post office. My parents would let me open the junk mail in answer to my "Is there something for me?" After we moved to Swan River, I loved it when a letter or package arrived with my name on it. Besides surprising me with the Reddi-wip dolls, Mum also arranged to have cards mailed to me from Bethlehem, Pennsylvania, with its special postmark at Christmas, and she ordered the free *Hinterland Who's Who* leaflets to arrive addressed to me.

However, an accumulation of dolls, leaflets, and special cards required storage, and we didn't have any. One month, Mum managed to squirrel away some extra cash and she showed me a photo of a metal shelving unit in the Sears catalogue. She measured and decided it would cover the entire end wall of her bedroom. The shelving would have been at home in Grandpa's workshop and not what one would consider fancy decor. No matter, it fit our price range. She asked if I thought we could put it together. I agreed we could and she placed the order.

I dragged the heavy box the two and a half blocks from the Sears pick-up office to our house. Mum and I spent the weekend with one of Daddy's screwdrivers building the structure. It looked like a production from an oversized Meccano set. We were very pleased with our efforts.

We joyfully discussed which books would be put on which shelf and whether we should store the board games on the top shelf or the bottom. Filling the metal shelves created space in Mum's room as boxes were finally emptied and the contents became more easily accessible. Sadly, we had more stuff to shelve than shelves and the sewing supplies remained boxed in my room beside Mum's treadle sewing machine.

On a cold winter evening, as Mum and I played our regular game of Scrabble, a horrendous crash in her room scared us half to death. In fear of what we might find, we opened the door to see that our metal shelving system had toppled over, scattering books, games, magazines, and craft supplies across Mum's bed and about the room. We didn't know metal shelving should be braced or anchored to the wall! We spent the rest of the evening gathering up books and trying to find all the pieces to puzzles and games, so Mum could go to bed. The next day when I arrived home from school, she proudly showed me her solution. She'd wrapped wire around a six-inch spike and hammered it into the wall. The ends of the wire were secured to the shelf uprights. The shelf never fell down again.

In many ways, "cheap" defined the '70s and, if you could make it yourself to save more money, even better. Hence, the plethora of bead curtains and macrame belts. I created a "chain" belt out of drink can pull tabs that I saw in a magazine and I proudly wore it to school to accessorize my jeans.

In an attempt to make our lives more comfortable while spending as little as possible, Mum decided we needed another chair. The only comfortable chair in the house sat beside the telephone, and whoever needed to use the phone got to sit in the chair. If the phone rang and the person in the chair answered a call intended for someone else, the chair had to be vacated in favour of the lucky call recipient.

We turned to the Sears catalogue again, where basket chairs—a conical wicker basket with narrow-gauge wire legs—were on sale. As a bonus of the sale, the buyer could choose two padded covers instead of one. Mum had the money, and we each chose our favourite cover pattern from the options. The beauty of this arrangement was that a dirty cover could be replaced with a clean one while the first got washed. Or, if you just wanted something fresh for a change of season, you could switch out the covers. Once again, I lugged our purchase home from the Sears office. I had to make two trips: one for the basket and the legs and one for the two covers. The chair didn't come put together. Again, Daddy's screwdriver came out of his toolbox to attach the legs to the basket. We were thrilled. It meant we each had a comfortable chair. We still did the telephone shuffle, but at least the person vacating the easy chair had a comfortable spot to land. We chose covers in hot pink corduroy and a tropical print in avocado and brown. When not in use, the chair created a bright spot in the dark room.

One day, I arrived home from school to find our chair crumpled on the floor. Apparently, Mrs. W., one of Mum's more rotund friends had come to visit and she had been offered the basket chair for comfort. The spindly wire legs promptly collapsed under her. The chair had not come with a weight limit warning! We straightened the legs as best we could but, until the chair was finally consigned to the backyard garbage pickup, it listed sideways whenever anyone sat in it.

*Dad brought Rosalie a spoon rack that he
had made. It holds fifty-four spoons and she had
thirty-four on it. Rosalie is so happy with it.*

---

*Daddy came and brought the old rocking chair looking
like new. I often wondered if it would be usable again.*

I finally worked Dad's "nutty" puzzle.

As a child, I believed my creative grandparents could solve any problem. In the days before internet searches and online videos to explain how to fix a broken lamp or piece of furniture, they used logic and ingenuity to devise a solution. I truly believe I benefited from living in close proximity to these clever people.

When we visited Wildwood, I shadowed Grandpa whenever I didn't have to help pick berries or shell peas or do any other chore assigned to me. He patiently explained what he needed to do to fix Grandma's sewing machine and how to do it. He taught me how to hammer a nail and explained the process he undertook to smoke moose meat. Grandpa lined up cans on fence posts and taught me to shoot his .22 caliber gun because he believed all girls in the country should know how to handle a firearm.

Grandpa constructed the cupboards and bookcases at Wildwood, and Grandma painted them. She sewed the curtains for the windows and the slipcovers to hide the worn upholstery on the easy chairs. Grandpa repaired furniture if it broke and he cut glass to replace shattered windows. Only when it was beyond fixing would a piece of furniture be thrown out. Purchasing a new item needed careful thought and discussion. Replacing an old couch in the living room in the late-1960s with a newly popular hide-a-bed—considered a major purchase—was not a decision made lightly. My grandparents would be horrified at the amount of waste in the world today and how disposable furniture has become. They could lead classes on how to recycle. Redecorating meant choosing a different paint colour for the walls; everything else stayed the same. Curtains had to be faded or frayed before Grandma purchased fabric and sat at her sewing machine to make replacements. Grandpa made wiping rags out of the discarded tattered curtains to mop up messes when he changed the oil in their car. I own a quilt Grandma made using pieces of men's wool underwear for its middle layer.

Grandpa's hand in my ambitious last 4-H project got me top marks from the local home economist. "She's just like her mother," the arbiter of all things expertly done told Mum's friend, Mrs. D, who had joined us at my achievement day. Mum helped me design a bedspread, curtains, toss cushions, and other items to decorate my room. She offered me her rocking chair, with its flat rockers (the result of her perpetual rocking), suggesting I make matching cushions for it. I solicited Grandpa's aid to get the chair rocking again. He chose sturdy, hard ash wood to make new rockers in his workshop. Then, he helped me strip the old varnish off the chair. Searching his workshop shelf, he found a can of stain in a tint he liked and showed me how to apply it to the wood. He guided me through the refinishing process using a partial can of varnish he also retrieved from his shelf. When restored, the chair looked like something I might have just purchased at the Co-op store.

For the same 4-H project, Grandpa made me a footstool to fit a piece of needlepoint. Over the years, he made countless footstools using the same standard design—four curved legs and a flat top. I sat on one of his footstools during our trip to Flin Flon in 1964. Mum gave her father the idea to make the top of my stool like a box. With my needlepoint complete, Mum helped me wrap it around a heavy piece of foam that could be pushed down into the box. She thought I might want to change the needlepoint in the future, but I never have. The rocking chair and the footstool have been part of my decor for decades wherever I have lived.

We are a family of collectors. In my grandparents' and parents' minds, a collection offered further education. We collected circular discs from Jell-O boxes with pictures of cars on them that doubled as Rummoli chips. I searched every new box of Red Rose tea that we drank by the potful for Wade figurines. Mum collected bells and stamps. We all collected coins, and Grandpa would let us go through his spare change in search of pennies to complete our coin books.

In the 1970s, souvenir spoons were small reminders of places visited or were brought back as gifts for family and friends. Encouraged by Mum and Grandma, I began collecting spoons. I saw an idea in a magazine for a rack in the shape of a US state to display spoons. I showed the design to Grandpa and he made a spoon rack for me in the shape of Manitoba! As one of the younger grandchildren who arrived as my grandparents eased into retirement, I had greater access to them. Any idea I had, Grandpa helped me make it or made it for me.

Grandpa loved the challenge puzzles presented. If he saw a puzzle in a magazine or at a friend's, he took note and made his own. On trips with Grandma, he picked up any new puzzle he saw. The Cracker Barrel restaurants in the United States are all about nostalgia, but there is an added hit of memory for me when I see Grandpa's favourite triangular puzzle on every table. I got so proficient at that one that I practised solving it with my eyes shut! Often, as we sat talking at the oak table, he would reach behind to a shelf that stored his stash of puzzles and put one down in front of me to solve.

Grandma's pottery and ceramic hobby eventually drew me in as well. Grandpa built Grandma a perfectly balanced pottery wheel and I tried my hand at throwing pots. Too young to master the process, I switched to building clay sculptures. I made two elephants—a candle holder, and a dust collector. Eventually, I just became a helper applying colour to simple items and adding glaze to already coloured and fired pieces.

Working with Grandma and teaching me gave Mum skills in pottery and ceramic production that helped her get a part-time job teaching pottery for the Swan River Recreation Department.

Many years later, I came to realize how being around creative, clever, problem-solving people had set me up with experiences that helped me get jobs, gave me knowledge to intelligently interview people from all walks of life from artists to zoologists, and instilled a determination to find answers to complex problems. Sadly, when we understand how parents and grandparents influence us, it's often too late to express our gratitude. I invoke their names to give them credit when I am complimented for using a skill I learned from Mum or my grandparents. It's the least I can do.

*Rosalie went to Rev. B's to babysit and got $1.75
(another piece of sheet music if she wants it).*

---

*Rosalie went to B's to babysit and earned $2.50. She
should soon have some money to spend for Christmas.*

---

*I took apart a little lime green Fortrel dress that
I had made for Rosalie. I will use it in my quilt.*

MANAGING EVERY aspect of our lives frugally, Mum made or helped me make most of my clothes. Eventually, I began making her clothes. The 1970s introduced us to cheap polyester double-knit and poly-cotton that often went on sale in the Sears catalogue or at the local dry goods store. I convinced Mum she looked "cool" in a pantsuit. I made her matching outfits—a print tunic with a solid yoke and matching solid pants, which, for a woman who wore dresses in every season, warmed up winter walks for her. The polyester fabrics also didn't require the same finishing techniques as better-quality fabrics, so I could make her a top and pair of elastic waist pants in a weekend. Leftover scraps of fabric became quilts. She also tore apart clothing I outgrew and recycled the pieces into quilt blocks or rugs.

When I turned twelve, I began getting calls to babysit, giving me my own spending money. As older neighbours moved to apartments or accommodations geared for seniors, they sold their homes to young families, who appreciated having a sitter living next door or across the back lane. I could confidently count on jobs for both Friday and Saturday and, when I got a call to look after kids on a Sunday or a school night, I was thrilled. Just as when Edward made his own money, Mum let me keep the cash I earned. With my babysitting money, I bought items for us she deemed too expensive.

I tore the Breck shampoo advertisements out of *Redbook* and *Woman's Day* magazines Ila passed on to Mum. I wanted hair like the girls in the pictures, so I bought Breck shampoo with my babysitting wages. A fragrant change from our regular Rexall hair product, I don't know if the Breck shampoo made my hair look like the advertisements, but a teenage girl likes to dream.

Mum, a big fan of the Rexall annual penny sale, stocked up on shampoo, soap, and other staples when it was on. She'd send me to purchase the largest bottle for full price and then we'd get a second for a penny. If Mum had extra change, she might send me back during its run to pick up more of the sale items and, if we rationed them carefully, we often had enough to last us until the next sale. I used the Breck shampoo sparingly and alternately with the Rexall shampoo, making the more expensive bottle last longer. I sometimes washed and styled Mum's hair and would use the Breck shampoo. If she did her own hair, she wouldn't use my shampoo. I tried to convince her that she deserved to use the special shampoo as much as I did, but she was so accustomed to putting herself last, she wouldn't help herself to it.

Also with my babysitting money, I began a collection of 45 RPM records by my favourite singers and bands—Elton John, ABBA, the Partridge Family. My best friend "Jayne" and I joined the Capitol Record Club, splitting the ten albums we got for one dollar. In the two years we had to fulfill our obligation of buying a dozen more records at regular price, I think she purchased the majority. However, every babysitting job meant the possibility of adding to my growing record collection. I ordered sheet music from Tredwell's in Winnipeg to get piano arrangements for songs on the records I bought. It turned out I practised playing rock and roll more diligently than the Chopin or Schubert required by my piano lessons!

I never got an allowance like other kids because Mum didn't have any extra money to give me. If the children next door were going to the store to buy candy with their weekly fifty cents, I would ask Mum if I could go with them. When she asked if I wanted something for myself, I would be given the dime to buy a pack of gum or a chocolate bar. While the others happily spent all their weekly allowance on everything they wanted until none remained, I got to buy one thing if Mum had the money to give me.

Babysitting gave me my own money and I could buy two packs of gum, if I wanted, but I never did. Wisely, Mum cautioned me against spending every cent I earned. She insisted I save some of it in case I wanted something costing more. Even in our impoverished circumstances, she believed in having a "rainy day fund." About half of my babysitting money went into a piggy bank and eventually I had enough to open a bank account. Mum walked me to the bank to help me navigate my entry into high finance. That account was seed money for my education, though I had no clue how much I would need!

The unregulated babysitting workforce got paid poorly thanks to a word-of-mouth pay scale set by the parents paying the wages. I started at fifty cents per hour and, with experience and longevity in the "business," I eventually earned seventy-five cents per hour. Edward had made seventy-five cents per hour at his grocery store job several years before I started babysitting. I tried to get jobs at local stores, but I inherited Mum's timidity. It took all the courage I could muster to ask the owner of the dry goods store for an application to work for him. Returning with the completed paperwork involved stiffening my backbone again. I don't recall getting interviewed, but I know I didn't get hired. My nervousness prevented me from applying for serving jobs even though I had experience gained through 4-H and school catering jobs. I worried I would spill something on someone. So my high school job was babysitting.

I had regular clients and, being young, I had fun with the children because my energy matched theirs. Every night I worked, I would arrive home with a dollar or more. Sometimes a good weekend, with clients who stayed out until the wee hours of the morning, would net me several dollars. With age and experience, I got on lists of potential sitters and I might get a call from someone new working down their list. Sitters also recommended each other. I got a really good job for New Year's Eve thanks to the referral of a friend who was already booked for the big night. The client was an officer of the Royal Canadian Mounted Police (RCMP) and, when my friend was busy, I became their second-choice sitter.

That particular New Year's Eve opportunity gave Mum a good story to tell, but worried her as well. While his wife got ready to go out and prepared their children for the evening, the officer headed to our house to pick me up. On the way, he got summoned to the detachment office.

I received a phone call from him close to my pickup time telling me not to worry because he was sending a squad car to fetch me. A few minutes later, an RCMP squad car with two officers in it pulled up in front of our house. One of the uniformed officers came to the door to ask for me. I grabbed my coat and bag containing the activities that would keep me awake until my clients got home and headed to the car. The officer opened the back door for me and I hopped in. I thought the whole thing an adventure. But, when she looked out the front door window, Mum got a little worried. What would the neighbours think when they saw her daughter being taken away in the back of a police car? It wouldn't have been the first time that a kid on our block got picked up in a police car but, in their case, they weren't going to a babysitting job.

During my drive across town, a message from my client came over the radio. "Did you pick up the package?" he asked.

The reply: "Affirmative."

Having never been in a police car before, I experienced some shock when I tried to get out of the car at my client's mobile home and couldn't find the door handle! But having a good-looking police officer open the door for me made me feel special. When I told Mum the story about my "delivery" the next morning, she relaxed and saw the incident as an opportunity to tell her friends how her daughter became a "package" of the RCMP. I think she also felt a little proud that her daughter babysat for a police officer. I didn't normally get calls from that level of client.

Until I started babysitting myself, I had no personal knowledge of sitters. I had never had a babysitter because one of my siblings stayed home to be with me. After they left home, Mum took me with her everywhere unless she thought the destination unsuitable for me and then she opted to stay home. She did not feel she had money to pay sitters. Other people in town did not share Mum's sense of parental responsibility. Even if they had low income, they figured out how they could go out while ensuring their children were looked after. My fifty-cents-per-hour jobs were most often thanks to those clients. My RCMP New Year's Eve job paid one dollar per hour, which included a twenty-five-cent bonus for the high-demand evening. Jobs like that didn't happen often. I knew we needed the money, so I took most jobs even for poor pay.

One babysitting job brought out Mum's "Mamma Bear" instincts. Her shyness prevented her from standing up for herself, but when it came to her children, Mum mustered her courage and fought for us. I babysat regularly for a client with three young boys all close in age. I don't remember the "Smith" family being particularly well-off, but they did like to go out. I usually sat for them at least one night per weekend. They paid me sixty cents per hour, so my per capita rate was just twenty cents per child! One Saturday, they called asking me to sit for them. The Smiths only lived about three blocks from us, so they did not pick me up as most of my clients did. There may have been an unwritten rule that if you lived across town you were picked up and brought home, but a few blocks' walk at 2:00 AM did not require a ride. When I arrived at the appointed time, I was introduced to another couple and their two boys. My client said I would be looking after all the kids while the adults went to a dance. With that, my workload increased, but I managed to wrangle all five boys, getting them fed, washed, and settled down to sleep.

When the two couples arrived back well after midnight, a discussion followed about whether I should be driven home. I opted to walk because I sensed some drunkenness. Mrs. Smith handed me payment for the time for her three boys. I expected the other mother would give me the same amount for babysitting her children. But my client turned to her friend, told her how much she had given me, and said the friend could pay her half later. Bottom line? I earned maybe four dollars for sitting five children from two families for the same payment I would normally get for sitting one child. Meanwhile, the parents had an evening out and paid a babysitter half what they would have paid had they each hired a sitter.

I arrived home and told Mum what had happened. The next time Mrs. Smith called to ask me to babysit, Mum took the call and told her I would never babysit for her again. Mum's interference left me miffed because I wanted any money I could get, even from a cheap client. Mum explained exploitation and the importance of standing up for my rights. Meanwhile, she would spend sixteen hours crocheting a doily for some rich lady in town and accept payment of five dollars. I wish Mum could have developed a stiffer backbone or that I could have helped her overcome her timidity in the way she helped me. But her shy personality and years of family conditioning to do as asked or accept her lot in life kept her in limbo between being a pushover and plucky.

I used my babysitting wages to help Mum but, other than buying food or fabric to make her clothes or fancy shampoo, it never occurred to me that I could also help keep the house standing. I could have given Mum some money here and there to help pay for furnace oil or to hire an electrician to repair the light fixture in my room, but I didn't. Of course, Mum would never ask and my three dollars earned on a Friday night babysitting job would have been a drop in the bucket in terms of our financial needs. Nevertheless, I am forlorn that I never saw our situation more clearly.

*I always miss the children and
think of them so often.*

---

*I can only strive towards helping
others to have happiness.*

---

*[Rosalie] bought me a new dish pan and it
certainly made doing the dishes easier. She also
brought me two storybook buttons—one with
a butterfly and one with an apple—very pretty.*

BEING A TEENAGER is a lot like walking through a crop infested with cleavers. Like the weeds' tendrils that wrap around other plants choking their growth, ideas both good and bad wrap around the adolescent brain, sometimes stunting the ability to recognize the difference. On one hand, I became more aware of our situation, yet I also fell victim to outside influences as I navigated towards adulthood.

I did develop an inkling of how Mum struggled, as demonstrated by the gifts I bought her. When she baked and needed to put crushed nuts in a recipe, she sat at the table and, using a knife, chopped the nuts on a cutting board. One Christmas, I gave her a nut chopper she could fill with nuts then push a plunger up and down so a blade inside would pulverize the nuts. In a minute, she would have all the walnuts or pecans chopped that she needed and some for the next recipe. I bet she pounded out some of her frustration using her new tool! I bought her a new cooking pot once because our only aluminum saucepan was getting pitted. Despite my childish efforts, I never made the connection between our one old pot and the fact that we had no money. I never wondered why Mum didn't replace the worn-down saucepan that flavoured everything cooked in it with a slightly metallic taste.

Edward had a greater understanding of Mum's needs. He arrived home for a visit with an Electrolux vacuum that Mum used for thirty years. Edward and Lynette also bought us a television! Uncle Billie gave us a big old television when I was about ten, and Mum had to scrape together the money to install an aerial on our roof. I know why Uncle Billie was getting a new television. Every program we watched on that set, we viewed through a haze of snow. So, the small black and white television from my siblings came as a wonderful surprise. Mum and I would play Scrabble while watching old movies she had seen when they were new in the theatres.

I never tested the rules as a teenager. I happily stayed home on a Friday evening with Mum, experiencing the same joy I had when hanging out with my friends. Unlike Edward, who would hitch a ride to a dance in Bowsman and then call Mum at 10:55 PM asking if he could stay out until midnight, knowing full well he couldn't make it home should she demand he honour his 11 PM curfew, I usually told Mum what time I would be home and I'd often be early.

Looking back, I can imagine her shock when I suddenly withdrew from her and became critical of our situation. She tried to learn what upset me, but I couldn't admit that someone close to us had undermined our relationship by blaming her for our poor living situation. Instinctively, I must have known that telling her would be hurtful. Instead, I became a sullen teenager. My negative attitude adjustment came courtesy of one of my aunts, who offered to buy me a Coke at the Co-op store cafeteria on a chilly winter Saturday when I was seventeen. As we sat sipping our drinks, she launched into a critique of my mother.

"I know you think the world of your mother," she began. "But she has her failings and it's time you faced them."

I felt stunned and I must have looked it.

"Your mother could've done more with that house," she continued. "She could've done a better job keeping it tidy. There's no excuse for books stacked on chairs."

"But we don't have enough shelves," I pointed out.

"Maybe you should get rid of some books." The thought of getting rid of books horrified me and I must have looked aghast.

"You'll be leaving home soon, and someday you'll have your own house. I'm telling you right now that if I ever visit you and see you living in a mess like your mother's, I'll tell you in no uncertain terms to clean it up and I'll wait right there for you to do it."

In shock, I went home and saw our house through my aunt's eyes: books and newspapers heaped on a chair beside the telephone, Mum's knick-knacks and her Tapestry Rose china stacked precariously in the china cabinet Grandpa made her, my sewing machine open and piled with my latest project, the vacuum cleaner sitting by the unused front door. It suddenly seemed like a horrible place to live. In my bedroom, clothing draped over a chair, because the closet could not hold more than a half dozen items, made me feel slovenly. Grabbing a glass from the pantry, I saw our everyday dishes piled on the narrow shelves like leaning towers that could topple at any second. Suddenly, I began silently reproaching Mum for our crowded, decrepit living space.

While we continued to play Scrabble and visited friends together, I quit sharing stories about what happened at school. I was never rude and I answered her questions, but I didn't volunteer information and I let her tell me her news as she filled the void of my silence. If I wasn't babysitting, I initiated plans with friends so I wouldn't be home. I quit inviting friends to come to the house and, instead, met them at the Dairy Queen or the movie theatre. If Jayne got her parents' car for the night, I ran out to the curb and waited instead of having her come to the door. I even began staying with a cousin on weekends occasionally. I knew I was avoiding Mum, but I couldn't tell her why and, on some level, I think I deluded myself into thinking she didn't notice.

But she did and she confided in Edward that my changed behaviour worried her. During a visit to Swan River, Edward took me aside and asked me what had gotten into me. I mumbled, "Nothin'."

"Look, whatever's bugging you isn't good," he replied to my stubborn muteness. "Just talk to her!" But I never did.

Instead, I planned my escape. I dreamed about getting away and going to university where I would live in a tidy dorm room. I thought about having a closet with a rail the width of the space instead of a tiny cubby with a few hooks. I thought about having a light in my room and maybe even a reading lamp. In my current situation, I could only escape to my room to read during daylight hours on weekends.

When I did leave home, I received weekly letters from Mum full of family news and encouragement. But I know now that my refusal to stay with her when I went home hurt her terribly. I didn't go home for Christmas in my first year at university, using the excuse that I had no money for a plane ticket. While that was partly true, I probably could have scraped together the money or perhaps Lynette or Edward would have loaned me the fare. Instead, I took the bus to Toronto and spent the holidays with a cousin. Eventually, living on my own without the influence of family gradually cleared my head and I began to understand Mum's struggles and her lessons. I also missed her. I wrote her long letters telling her about my new experiences and, when I had a little extra money, I phoned her. When I mentioned in a letter that my ears got cold walking to class, she used what little money she had, likely at the expense of not getting something she needed, to buy yarn to make me a toque and paid the postage to mail it to me.

In today's world, we would have been encouraged to go for counselling, but that wasn't even a "thing" in small-town Manitoba in the 1970s. So I left and The Hovel was never my home again. Mum, who had complained bitterly about that house from the moment the family moved into it, inadvertently gave me reasons to leave it. Mum's dislike of the house transferred to me over the years and, thanks to the unkind words of an aunt, I saw the failings of the house—too small, no storage, useless kitchen—as her failings. I couldn't wait to get away from her and it.

To make our uncomfortable situation worse, and before I could put my escape plan in action, Mum made a dramatic decision that put us on a different path. I wish I could tell her how sorry I am that I wasn't there for her when things went horribly wrong. Especially when I know that she never ever let me down the way I did her.

THE HAUNTED ACRES

The day of Naomi's second marriage, before the move to The Haunted Acres. From left to right: Lynette, Rosalie, Naomi, and Edward. Edward's daughters, Tracy and Shelley, join the group in the photo.

*Yesterday a lady came and got me to fill
out a form for a library course and I had all the
qualifications but one—too much education.
It was for people with nine grades or under.*

*Twenty-nine years ago today, Danny and
I were married and we were so happy.*

THE SUMMER before I started Grade 12, Mum remarried. I don't know why. Maybe the prospect of being alone after I finished high school worried her and she got an offer that would save her from the anticipated loneliness. The marriage happened as she finally made progress toward getting out from under the welfare cloud.

Intended to help people gain skills and, potentially, get them off social assistance, retraining opportunities were introduced in the 1970s. Mum never lost her speed or accuracy on manual typewriters, but the new electric models required a lighter touch. Developing the habit of hitting a return key rather than reaching for a lever, and becoming accustomed to the sensitivity of the keys, proved challenging to all of us who had learned on manual machines. Mastering the electric typewriter would give Mum a marketable skill and, she was told, increase her chances for employment. Most of the retraining courses were offered at the high school because it had shops and laboratories to teach trades—auto repair, forestry management, secretarial skills. I thought I might feel odd meeting Mum going into typing class as I exited mine but, if it helped her get a job, I figured I could adjust.

While retraining opportunities were identified for Mum and she went through the application and selection process, the town recreation department hired her on a casual basis to teach pottery and ceramics to bored doctors, stay-at-home moms, and seniors. During her time teaching and babysitting a kiln full of learners' efforts in another low remuneration job, she met the man she would marry. The recreation director insisted the kiln, located in the local arena, be attended whenever in use, but didn't pay extra for her sitting alone all day beside a brick furnace. The custodian of the arena began chatting with her while she sat placidly crocheting to pass the time. Soon he sent her flowers and took her to eat in restaurants—a novelty for her. They went for drives in the country, a favourite pastime of our family that had ended with Daddy's death. As they toured around the countryside, he patiently stopped, allowing her to take photos of roadside flowers. They dropped in on her parents unannounced, something she had not been able to do for a decade. While she continued to mourn my father, this new man made her feel special.

When he proposed and she accepted, her life came to a screeching halt. The offer to train her on an electric typewriter was withdrawn. A program teaching library cataloguing got dropped because she now had a man to look after her. She told me years later, she wanted to do the secretarial retraining before she got married, but my stepfather talked her out of it saying she wouldn't need a job. An empty promise. Her marriage ended our reliance on the welfare system, restoring some of Mum's pride. But worse was yet to come.

I won't put his name in print because I want to minimize his existence in our lives. He turned out to be a mental and emotional abuser, and he even threatened to strike her once. She told me she stood her ground and he backed off. I am proud of her for not allowing the abuse to get physical. I think it shows a strong sense of self-worth that, despite the life challenges Mum faced, she did not believe she deserved his disrespect. Nevertheless, she still put up with a lot during a marriage that lasted less than three years.

A widower, with two adult children not much older than my seventeen years, he courted my mother in storybook fashion. After the marriage ended, rumours began to swirl about his temper and how he may have caused his first wife's heart attack. Mum wondered why they had not surfaced during the courtship. I don't know if she loved him, because her heart truly belonged to my father. I do believe she enjoyed his company and he made a good show of sharing her interests in the beginning. If they went to the local drive-in restaurant for milkshakes, he would tell her to order an extra for me. Arriving home from a babysitting job, I would find a lukewarm beverage waiting for me that I did not enjoy. His kindness toward me mattered to her, but it turned out to be a mirage that disappeared after their wedding.

I learned about blended families by reading Jayne's teen magazines. I followed advice to view him as Mum's new partner and not as a replacement for Daddy because there could be no such thing. According to the magazines, Mum's new relationship had no bearing on my missing parent. I do admit, I didn't like him. Instinctually, I felt he was shifty, but not in a criminal way. I didn't trust his attempts to earn my regard because they seemed false. But I didn't know how to put my concern into words. I just knew he wasn't anything like my grandfather and family friends who looked out for us. I wonder, had I been able to find a way to voice my indistinct distrustful feeling instead of deciding to be supportive, she might have refused him. I will never know.

The marriage and move to a new house outside of town made the house Mum and I shared excess. But retaining ownership of our house in town worked well for me. I began taking the bus to school but, if I had any after-school activities, the bus left the school without me. 4-H, volunteering as a candy-striper, and babysitting meant I spent many evenings in town. If my obligation didn't begin until 7:00 PM, I went to our house and did my homework until I had to be somewhere.

Getting to our new country home when I stayed in town required energy and ingenuity. I walked in warmer months and could take a shortcut across the river via a swinging bridge. I didn't like crossing the bridge but it shaved almost a kilometre off my walk. Without the shortcut, I would have to take the main road and its sturdier bridge. Sometimes I could wait at our house in town until my stepfather finished work and then he would take me home. By Grade 12, Jayne had her own car and lived in the same direction from town and, if we went to the movies or were staying late at school, she gave me a ride.

My stepfather encouraged Mum to sell The Hovel. He began bringing real estate agents to meet her in an attempt to initiate a listing. To her credit and ultimate safety, Mum held fast and didn't get around to selling. He didn't want to move her belongings to his house, but she wasn't keen on ditching items it had taken her years to collect—books, Christmas ornaments, her craft supplies. Their deliberations over the move and selling her house reached a stalemate. In the end, the house Mum hated became her deliverance.

*Had one of those realistic dreams about Danny
last night and awoke crying. He said that he wouldn't
be able to come to see me anymore because I was being
married. I don't see how a dream can seem so real.*

THE COUNTRY PROPERTY purchase happened after Mum accepted the marriage proposal. First, they planted a large garden on the small acreage. Mum loved having a garden again. In the first blush of courtship, my mother referred to the property as "The Acres." Eventually she changed the moniker to "The Haunted Acres." It is a mere blip in my memory of the houses I inhabited.

The Haunted Acres is a perfect example of "be careful what you wish for." Mum imagined her dream house would be decorated with quilts and doilies, and have comfortable furniture and many bookshelves. She envisioned hosting Women's Institute meetings and having friends to tea in a nice home. She got her dream home, but it became a nightmare.

He said she could design a house for the property and, although small, Mum realized all her ideas for a home—a bay window, built-in bookcases, display shelves, rooms with colour. Her kitchen had a new full-sized fridge, a good stove, a working sink, and enough cupboards to store her sizable collection of cake pans, cookie cutters, pots, baking dishes, and supplies. But moving to the country meant her part-time, casual jobs ended because people didn't bring their cakes to her to be decorated or ask her to do baking. Her husband turned out to be a miser. He paid the bills and gave her a household allowance, but she didn't have any cash of her own to spend.

The clean, dry, unfinished basement at The Haunted Acres contained a brand-new appliance for Mum and me. My stepfather brought home a combination washing machine and extractor and hooked it up in the basement. The washing drum and extractor were not always one unit as they are now. Mum and I figured out how to use the little machine then hung our clothes on an outdoor line or, in winter, on a cable strung in the basement. One day as I headed downstairs with an armload of washing, including my new burgundy hip hugger cords, my stepfather stopped me in the kitchen.

"Are you doing a wash?" he asked. "If you are, can you do some for me?"

How could I say no? I don't remember the number of items he gave me, but the pile included the long johns he wore for work under his uniform. I read my book while the washer sloshed the laundry around and, when it stopped, I slopped it into the extractor and spun the water out. Afterwards, I hung everything on the line in the basement. I collected my clothes when they were dry and never gave the chore another thought.

The next day, my distraught mother came to my room and explained I needed to apologize to my stepfather for shrinking his wool long johns. When he discovered my misdeed, he yelled at Mum about her stupid child. He should have been happy I shrank them because the dye in my burgundy cords ran, colouring his precious long johns pink. I don't think he would have liked wearing pink underwear! I apologized to him and he asked how dumb I had to be to wash wool in hot water. It seemed pointless to explain I had no knowledge of wool care because I only wore the cheapest polyester or cotton. He never asked me to do his laundry again.

I believe the cracks in the marriage began to appear on the honeymoon, which he told Mum to plan. They toured through the United States stopping to visit relatives and friends of both. He soon began to berate Mum for her "begging." Mum hid her shyness by seeking topics of mutual interest when she met new people. During one visit at his relatives', the host learned he and Mum shared a passion for stamp collecting. As the newlyweds were leaving, the host gave her an envelope of stamps for her collection. According to Mum, my stepfather accused her of asking for the stamps. When they reached Pennsylvania and Mum's family, who generously took them out to eat and gave them gifts, he accused Mum, again, of begging and taking advantage of her kin. "I couldn't wait to get home," she said.

Got up in the night and what an experience! Bumped into a chair and thought I would end up in the river—[he] left the "picture frame" on the toilet up and I never turn on a light. The price one pays for having a man around the house!

DESPITE HAVING a comfortable, warm house, Mum's life became even more restricted. Her only possession of any value sat empty and unheated in town. My stepfather's desire to sell her house as quickly as possible may have been his way of getting control of the little wealth she had. They didn't have a joint bank account so the money from the sale would have ended up in his possession. Because he worked for the town, he knew its zoning and development plans. He assured her she would get a good price because the location of the house gave it ideal access to the town's services and shopping area—the reason Grandpa had pressured Mum into the house years earlier. Mum's reticence to let go of our house may have contributed to the end of the marriage, but she also may have been silently comparing him to my father. My stepfather and his anger and insecurity came up short in the comparison.

My stepfather childishly demanded Mum give an accounting of what she bought with the household allowance. Because she didn't drive, she couldn't get to town without him and he had to take her shopping or to visit friends, a situation he grew to resent. Stuck at The Haunted Acres, she lost her Scrabble dates with our neighbour and tea with friends.

Teaching me to drive before the marriage eased the strain of isolation for us and turned out to be one of his rare kindnesses. However, he couldn't contain his annoyance during parallel parking practice when I slid into a snowbank and put a small dint in his right fender. Once I passed my driver's test, he let me borrow his Dodge Dart to take Mum to town on weekends, providing he wasn't using the car to go visit his friends or family.

My life radically changed for good and ill that year. I got my own room to decorate. Mum helped me wallpaper a corner of it with red flocked paper popular in the 1970s. The L-shaped room, with a dormer window wide enough to fit my sewing machine, became my haven. I had a half wall of bookshelves, a decent closet, and a new bed. My new room at The Haunted Acres became the canvas for my final 4-H project. Having a room of my own meant I could have friends over to listen to records like any other teenager.

Safe in my space in the house's second storey, I was oblivious to the unravelling relationship on the floor below. Arguments in the main floor master bedroom were muffled while I listened to my growing collection of 45s. When the house got quiet, I knew my stepfather had gone to work or was off visiting his family.

My babysitting jobs gradually disappeared after our move outside of town. In-town parents didn't want to drive back and forth to the country. I had a regular job during the winter babysitting two children across the street from The Hovel while their parents played in a weekly curling league. I relied on the money I earned every week and tried to keep the job despite our move. After school, I waited in our cold and dark house until I could cross the street to their warm bungalow, spending a few hours with the children. But the father had to drive me home and he made comments about having to drive so far—about two kilometres. One night, I could tell he was quite drunk and I told Mum when I got home. She immediately began to worry about my safety. As long as we lived across the street, a few after-game beers weren't an issue because they walked to and from the curling rink. Once I moved, keeping me as their sitter lost its appeal and, with Mum's urging, I quit my last regular babysitting job.

Most of the places I frequented in town were contained within two square kilometres and were easily accessible from The Hovel. Once Mum remarried, our life became cramped. Her new husband, who seemed happy to go for drives around the Swan River Valley every weekend before they married, suddenly complained that he couldn't afford gas in the car. Mum had to turn down a job teaching a pottery class in Cowan, roughly fifty kilometres away, because he said he couldn't afford the wear and tear on his car to drive her there. As I lost babysitting jobs, Mum's supplemental income disappeared, too. The only personal money she had came from the last cake decorating jobs booked before the move.

The glaringly one-sided financial arrangements gave him power. He told her he couldn't afford gas to take her to visit her parents. Meanwhile, he flaunted his cash by buying himself a fancier skill saw or a bigger lawnmower.

With a new house, Mum wanted to take her turn hosting family celebrations. Our family decided to gather at The Haunted Acres for one of the holiday meals. Excited to display her home, Mum began to plan. In uncharacteristic bonhomie, my stepfather welcomed the opportunity to show off to his new in-laws. But someone in the family insisted on switching the celebration to either my aunt's acreage or my uncle's farm, leaving Mum hurt and disappointed. Making the situation worse my stepfather berated her about her horrible, ignorant, selfish family. She told me she cried for days from the fallout of the altered plan.

Luckily for me, I spent less time there than Mum. After the marriage in the summer of 1975, Lynette suggested I come stay with her in Winnipeg until the start of my last year of high school, and she helped me get a job pumping gas. At full-time minimum wage, I made more money than I ever had babysitting! I saved as much as I could toward my university tuition. Lynette didn't charge me rent even though she could probably have used the help. I bought groceries and cooked, and I sewed clothes for her in an attempt to pay my way.

That summer in Winnipeg got me thinking about my dissatisfaction with Mum. The new tidy house with our belongings stored on shelves and in closets fit our joint vision of "house beautiful." It could have been a bridge for us because it showed her ability to maintain a tidy, organized home. However, the mother, stepfather, teenager triangle made any form of resolution difficult while Mum tried to appease her new husband and deal with a stubbornly silent daughter.

When I went back to Swan River for Grade 12, Mum had moved to The Haunted Acres. I tried to settle into our new life while making plans to be gone as soon as I finished high school. My graduation caused another crack in the marriage. Mum wanted to give me a graduation gift and convention would suggest that I would receive one gift from both of them. Instead, he took the opportunity to cruelly upstage her.

I fell in love with a red watch at the local jewellery store and Mum suggested that could be my graduation gift. He said she could do what she wanted, but didn't offer to help with the cost. She had enough money from decorating someone's wedding cake and told me to buy the watch.

The following Saturday, my stepfather asked me to accompany him to town because he wanted to get me something for my graduation. We went to the same store and he told me to pick out a watch. I suggested maybe something else because Mum had just given me a watch. He told me to choose a watch or nothing. Confused and not wanting to anger him, I picked a simple inexpensive watch. Annoyed, he told me to pick something in the seventy-dollar range. I stood aside while he paid for a delicate silver watch with tiny diamonds sparkling near the face. When we got home, he instructed me to show Mum the gift he got me. Mum never showed any hurt over his one-upmanship. When I told her how uncomfortable the transaction made me, she said I had chosen a lovely watch and that I should wear it and enjoy it. Instead, I wore the watch she gave me because, even though it cost a tiny fraction of my stepfather's gift, it ticked with love.

With graduation nearing, I waited for my ticket out of Swan River and off to my new life at journalism school. When a letter arrived telling me I hadn't been accepted, I realized with horror that I might be stuck in Swan River indefinitely. Poor guidance from a counsellor at school proved to be my undoing. She encouraged me to put all my eggs in one basket and only apply to Ryerson Polytechnic, as the university was called then. Ryerson turned my application down because I didn't appear for a personal interview as required. I had submitted the alternative, a personal essay explaining why I wanted to attend the School of Journalism, because I didn't have the money to pay for a trip to Toronto. Apparently, my essay was received, but prospects who appeared for the interview must have been more favourable.

"Crushed" best describes how I felt. I knew I needed to get a job and I envisioned a future making minimum wage at one of the grocery stores while some stranger became the next star reporter at the local weekly paper. I also saw myself trapped at The Haunted Acres witnessing a crumbling marriage and suffering the diminishing tolerance of my stepfather.

Edward came to my rescue, suggesting I move to Thompson and hunt for a job there. I took up residence on his family's couch but, after two or three months with no success, I returned south. Auntie Rene offered me a room in her house in The Pas, where she and Lynette were both working. I got work and, thanks to my family, I saved almost enough to pay for one year of university, reducing my reliance on the student loan system. My aunt, a teacher and counsellor, got me on track with my applications. She insisted I apply to the University of Manitoba, where provincial residents had a good shot at acceptance. My high school counsellor wasn't there to talk me out of it so I applied to my first choice of Carleton University in Ottawa. I did not apply to Ryerson again. Both applications were successful, but I chose Carleton. I ordered a big steamer trunk from Sears, packed it with clothing, a blanket from a cousin reducing her wedding gift inventory, and new towels Mum had been saving for guests we never welcomed. Another cousin dropped the trunk at the train station to be shipped to Carleton's student residence and I left all the houses of my childhood behind me.

Without me there as a witness, Mum's situation became worse. My stepfather no longer needed to maintain an appearance of kindness, so he relaxed into his normal personality. Mum became stranded at The Haunted Acres, isolated from her friends with no money and no relief.

Finally, at the urging of her doctor, who feared for her safety, Mum moved back to The Hovel. In hindsight, it's good she waffled about selling it. But, if her life was a struggle after Daddy's death, it became worse when her second marriage ended. She now had no money. Retraining opportunities were not available without the recommendation of the welfare office and, too embarrassed by her failed marriage, she wouldn't apply for social assistance. Uncle Henry came through and gave her money he claimed he owed her. Mum used some of the cash to buy paint, wallpaper, and carpet ends to finally spruce up the house that had been in the same sorry state for over a decade. Two of her good friends helped her with the decorating.

Despite her reduced circumstances, she was happy. If possible, she lived even more frugally. But, again, fate and her father intervened. Grandma began to exhibit odd behaviour and it became apparent that she was in the middle stages of dementia. Grandpa didn't want to put his wife of nearly sixty years in care. He asked Mum to join him at Wildwood to look after her mother. As Grandma's mind declined, Uncle Henry arrived home with a cancer diagnosis. He hated hospitals and asked Mum if she would be his caregiver. She became the full-time caregiver for two people with very different health issues. During the day, Mum helped her brother in and out of bed and coaxed him to eat. At the same time, she made meals for her parents and tried to distract Grandma from her penchant of taking off down the lane towards Pennsylvania.

Uncle Henry recognized that his sister's help saved him from care-giving strangers and possibly a lengthy decline in hospital. He paid Mum for her services and suggested their father should pay her as well. But Grandpa said it was her duty to care for her mother and didn't see the need to give her any compensation. After all, wasn't she living there for free and eating their food? Uncle Henry's generosity wasn't quite enough and Lynette took over paying Mum's taxes and other bills.

Grandma and Uncle Henry died within months of each other and Mum returned to The Hovel. Grandpa went to live with Auntie Rene. Mum managed to survive, with Lynette's continuing help, until she turned sixty-five and began getting the Old Age Pension. Oddly, that pension cheque gave Mum the most money she'd ever had in her life, exceeding the amount of the welfare cheque. Not accustomed to having extra money, Mum went to the bank and opened an account!

She achieved a long-held dream to travel. While she never left North America, she and a friend went on bus trips to the east coast and through the southern United States. She loved sending us postcards from places like Peggy's Cove and New Orleans and we loved getting them. While this period of having enough money to fulfil her dreams was short-lived, I am so happy she had a few halcyon years.

I no longer lived in Swan River and was shamefully oblivious to Mum's plight through the five or so years while her marriage unravelled and her older brother and mother declined. Many miles away, I didn't take responsibility for getting my piano moved back to The Hovel. Somehow she got it moved because she wouldn't leave it behind. After having many of her belongings given or taken away from her earlier in her life, she was committed to protecting our treasures. Wrapped up in my new world of university and becoming a more confident person than the timid, bullied schoolgirl I had been when I arrived with my trunk, I was unaware of how carefully she saved to buy yarn to knit me a lovely Aran sweater. On completion, she had to scrape together enough money for the postage to get it to me. I learned about the challenges she overcame later after I graduated and moved back to

Manitoba. We mended our disconnection, resuming long visits and marathon Scrabble games. Hearing about her hardships—like sleeping on a mattress on the floor beside Grandma's hospital bed in the living room at Wildwood to keep her mother in bed all night—gave me a host of mixed feelings. I felt so sorry for her plight and guilty that I had been too self-centred to realize she managed a situation most people would refuse. I admit, I felt some anger that my adored grandfather could treat his eldest daughter so shabbily. I also directed some hatred at the universe in general that my kind, sweet mother could be so ill-used throughout her life. But I also admire her sturdy commitment to never complain and to always do her best to help and support family or friends in need.

Mum continued to inhabit the house she always hated. In a weird twist of fate, like her mother before her, dementia began to dull her memory. Sadly, the building that symbolized all of our struggles as a poor family became the only refuge she knew. Even though she argued with Grandpa about it not meeting our needs, it became the one place she remembered as a home. When we moved Mum into a seniors apartment complex, she walked back to that house almost every day to sit in the cold and dark. She didn't know where else to go. She finally had a warm bachelor suite with a decent bathroom and a good refrigerator, but she couldn't appreciate it. We supplied new towels for her lovely bathroom but, when I visited, she'd brought the old worn towels—the ones acquired with detergent labels—from The Hovel to use.

Eventually, Mum's health declined badly and we had to move her to Winnipeg. The Hovel remained behind and she repeatedly asked when she could go home. She could not understand that its deteriorated condition made it unliveable.

The Hovel sat neglected until we could sell it after Mum died. It got broken into. The basement continued to flood. With no heat on or hydro and the water turned off, the house decayed. I didn't shed a tear when it went under the wrecking ball. We salvaged some of its finer points—the stained glass windows, the solid wood doors, the vintage light fixtures—and we use them to decorate our houses today. I see these items not as reminders of an unfortunate chapter in our lives, but as symbols of our resilience as a family. They remind me of Mum, whose struggles never got in the way of her love and support for us.

WILDWOOD

Edward and Rosalie in the yard at
Wildwood, showing off his Parisienne.

*We went to the folks after chores were finished.
Grandpa was ready with his movie camera
to take pictures of us all. Some were of Danny and
Henry sawing the [frozen] moose in half and Edward
and Harley carrying a [frozen] turkey to the house.*

WHILE I VIEW my grandfather's treatment of Mum as insensitive and decry the challenges we faced in our various houses, Wildwood remained a constant in my life. The property remains in the family and is now farmed by a cousin. I never visit it anymore. If I had to draw a picture of Wildwood, it would be a happy illustration using warm colours. The family is spread across the province, but on occasion, when we gather, talk inevitably centres on the good times we had at Wildwood.

For all of us, the house shone brightest at Christmas. Once our individual celebrations were over Christmas morning, the families converged on Wildwood. Grandpa had a small movie camera and he stood in the cold outside the door filming each family arriving at the farm Christmas morning. If we walked too fast as we rushed toward the house, eager to see family or to put presents under the tree or to keep dishes wrapped in blankets and towels from cooling off, he made us back up and walk slower.

Once in the house, the women bustled about the kitchen cutting turkey, piling mountains of mashed potatoes into serving bowls, and ferrying dishes wafting wonderful smells to the room-length dining room table. Purchased by my great-grandfather at an auction sale, the rectangular oak table had come with several leaves but Grandpa made two more to extend it even further. When one more leaf would cause the apparatus to collapse, he created an additional table out of sawhorses and plywood the exact height and width of its oak neighbour.

Besides my grandparents and their three married children, ten grandchildren rounded out the company. On the very rare Christmas Uncle Henry came home from his trapline, an occurrence I only remember the year Daddy died, he sat in his usual place on Grandpa's left. Grandma never left anyone alone for a holiday meal, inviting local bachelors to join us.

With steaming dishes of food set on the table, we assembled around it and Grandpa said grace. As we got older, he would delegate a grandchild to ask the blessing over the sumptuous meal. I remember memorizing a short grace Mum found in one of her *Ideals* magazines. She believed that the honour of saying grace over the family Christmas meal required something new and not our standard "For what we are about to receive, Dear

Lord, make us truly grateful." Thankfully, she sat beside me and, as my shyness took over, she prompted me to get through the short verse.

After a collective "Amen," the food started making the rounds of the table. Each family contributed something to the delicious meal. Auntie Rene supplied the bird because they raised turkeys. When they quit the turkey business, she continued to supply a massive bird each year. She can be seen on Grandpa's home movies carrying a gigantic roasting pan she had likely put in her oven in the wee hours of the morning. Sometimes Uncle Allan, her husband, carried the turkey. One year, Edward was commandeered to carry the bird and he pretended to slip and drop it when he got in front of Grandpa's lens. Auntie Cassie brought roasting pans full of perogies and cabbage rolls made with her own sauerkraut. Grandma supplied the vegetables—large bowls of fluffy mashed potatoes, her wonderful creamed corn, and a mixed dish of peas and carrots. Mum supplied the steamed Christmas pudding with sauce and a variety of holiday-theme cookies.

Jellied salads were all the rage through the 1960s and '70s. It's a memory of Christmas dinners at the farmhouse that Lynette and I share and one I discovered lodged in the memories of various cousins as well. Grandma insisted the holiday table had to have a red jellied salad and a green one. They were improved by the addition of a can or two of fruit cocktail. As time went on and fewer of us surrounded the table, she continued to insist on the two bowls of jelly even though one would have been plenty. Perhaps she couldn't decide which could be forgone, the red or the green. I hated getting a spoonful of the salad if it had a grape in it. I didn't like the taste or the feel of the fruit in my mouth. When my parents dished my plate, I could not choose what went on it. But, when I could be trusted to serve myself, I would surreptitiously dig around in the bowl to avoid getting a grape. I loved the cool jelly and the other fruit and wouldn't avoid the dish completely.

"I never liked the grapes," Vern told me when I asked him about his memories of Christmas. "I did like the jelly." We laughed that several decades have passed between Christmases at Wildwood and our present lives and we are just discovering we both disliked the grapes in Grandma's cherished jellied salads. I think she would be disconcerted to learn her important yuletide contribution was her grandchildren's least favourite dish.

Children never like to waste time eating. As soon as we met the rule of cleaning our plates, we could ask permission to leave the table. This involved getting the attention of Grandpa. First, we got the okay from a parent to leave our chair and walk the length of the table to Grandpa's place at the head and wait until he acknowledged our presence.

"Please, Grandpa, may I be excused?" Wringing my hands behind my back, I awaited his answer.

"Have you cleaned your plate?" he always asked.

"Yes, Grandpa."

"Did you enjoy your food?" he countered. "What did you like best?"

"It's all delicious, but I really like the cabbage rolls."

"Well, then, I guess you can be excused," he would say after getting a nod from a parent. Once released, with Grandma's blessing we retrieved the box of toys from her closet and headed upstairs to create new games or replay old ones. We could not hope to try any new board games we brought from home as long as the table was covered in food and surrounded by adults.

With the meal over and the food and used crockery taken to the kitchen, the fathers removed the leaves, dismantled the second table, and returned the chairs to their rightful places throughout the house, including my usual seat, the piano bench, to the front of the instrument. The mothers organized food storage and the process of hand washing the pile of dishes began. A line of dish driers waited their turn for glasses (always washed first), plates, serving dishes, and finally cooking pots. As we aged, we all joined this well-trained army of end-of-meal cleaners. We each had a job that, besides clearing the table, washing, and drying, included returning all the clean, dry items to storage.

Presents were handed out when the cleanup was complete. Gifts exchanged between families were often handmade stuffed toys for the children and gifts of food, like a venison roast or a turkey. Grandpa made a big ceremony of personally giving each family member five crisp one-dollar bills—our gift from both him and Grandma. He stood in front of each person and carefully counted out the amount to place in their hand. He enjoyed going to the bank to collect mint-condition paper currency with the serial numbers of the approximately one hundred notes in sequence. In 1967, Canada's centennial year, he surprised us with five shiny silver dollars that he retrieved from a cotton bank bag.

While the adults rested, the children played. If the games got rowdy or supper made the table off limits, we got shooed outside or to another part of the house. A cold, buffet-style supper offered delights we only saw once a year. Besides the makings for turkey sandwiches and a repeat offering of the red or green jellied salads, stuffed green olives, tinned smoked oysters, and Mandarin oranges were added to the mix. Grandpa made popcorn balls for Christmas and pull taffy in pink and green. Those treats, along with cookies or cake supplied by Mum and my aunts, were available for dessert. After the huge lunchtime meal, we enjoyed being allowed to nibble without the formality of sitting at the table. Our parents turned a blind eye to how many cookies we consumed as long as we ate everything we put on our plates. Food found uneaten on window sills or on the top of the desk resulted in an interrogation to reveal the guilty party. The identified offender endured a lecture about wasting food.

As the day wound to a close, Grandpa set up his movie projector, unfurled the screen, and showed us the movies of Christmases past. He spliced the annual films together and we never tired of watching the years scroll by. Each year was introduced with a shot of his plywood Santa holding a sign saying "Merry Christmas" and the year attached on a removable card. The silent home movies show the escalation of hemlines, the reduction of fins on cars, new coats and then those coats appearing on younger cousins, the height of the snowbank, the advancing ages of the people in the frames, and the last year Daddy appeared in the films.

One year, after Edward moved to Thompson, he bought himself a bright red two-door Parisienne that he proudly drove home for Christmas, chopping down a tree for us along the way. We had Christmas Eve as a family and decorated the tree together. On Christmas morning, after emptying our stockings and opening presents, we loaded Edward's car with gifts and food for the trip to the farm. Lynette and I settled in the back seat, and Mum rode shotgun. On our arrival at the farm, Grandpa rushed out of the house to get in position with his movie camera.

"Let's give him a show," Edward declared, as he drove into the yard. He then proceeded to rip some donuts around the large yard with Mum clutching the armrest and yelling, "Edward, what are you doing? Stop!" Grandpa got it all on tape. The next summer we were reminded of that joy ride because the grass was burned in large circles across the yard. It took all summer and part of the next year before the evidence of Edward's fun disappeared in new growth.

The house with its stucco walls and red brick corners is the backdrop for the celluloid Christmas records that we never tired of watching year after year. We loved seeing ourselves grow up. If my grandparents had visited family in the United States, there might be an interlude of summer scenes starring people we rarely saw. When the screen faded to black, leftovers were packed, the box of toys returned to Grandma's closet, and games and our belongings collected. We bundled into vehicles and left the house glowing behind us.

Wildwood anchored my childhood as a constant, unchanging refuge. After Daddy died, it became a sanctuary from our poorly insulated farmhouse that I mostly remember as dark and cold. When we moved to The Hovel, I never noticed the stark contrast between it and Wildwood until I began to lose my childhood innocence. By the time I reached high school, I began to see the cracks in our walls and compared them to my grandparents' blemish-free house. Mum's dislike of The Hovel finally rubbed off on me. I began to think of my grandparents' house, with its clever storage, backup heating and sewer options, generous living area, and room for a family to gather, as the ideal family home. The Haunted

Acres had the potential to compete in comfort and style with Wildwood, but its attributes were erased by my mother's disastrous second marriage.

Grandpa and Grandma were fortunate to have all their family living within a short drive of Wildwood. The home movies document the passage of time where, for over two decades, we spent glorious times at the best house in the district. After Grandpa died, a cousin lived in the house briefly and then abandoned it. Dereliction and lack of care eventually took its toll and what remains can no longer be seen behind the overgrown trees bordering the remnants of Grandma's garden. Few people in the district driving along the road remember the thriving family and the two wonderful people who welcomed everyone to their home. Made of logs and not brick, the house often kept my family safe from the wolves of life. Within its walls, I learned many skills and valuable lessons. I remember Wildwood as it was in my childhood and hold its warmth in my heart.

EPILOGUE

Rosalie had her interview today [with a guidance counsellor]. She said that she was asked what person influenced her life the most and she named me. "Who else has done as much?" I hope that I haven't failed her or any of them.

ACCOMPLISHED MY GOAL of completing university and then embarked on a journalism career that took me from Winnipeg to smaller communities around the province and then back to the city. When I began the search for my first apartment, I discovered I didn't like the more economical basement suites that people create to earn extra money and began skipping over the advertisements for these subterranean living options.

In one small town, the only vacancy was a three-bedroom townhouse that echoed when I walked through it because I didn't have any money to buy furniture. I set up a card table in one of the empty bedrooms and put my typewriter on it, passing the room off as an office. One bedroom contained my bed and a small dresser and the third remained empty as long as I lived there.

I found colourful living quarters in a glorified bachelor apartment under the third-floor eaves of a former bank. The main area contained wall-to-wall red-and-black indoor/outdoor carpet. The bed, fitted under the angle of the roof, mostly hid the olive-green carpet that was added when the red and black covering ran out.

As I progressed through my career, "paying my dues" and discharging my student debt, I could afford nicer accommodation. Eventually, I purchased a two-bedroom condo on the main floor of a building in a lovely compound. My unit overlooked a green space and I prepared myself to be content there. I planned to turn the second bedroom into a library and guest room. A large storage space that doubled as a laundry room would store my sewing supplies. I decided to revisit history and share my bedroom with a sewing machine.

But fate intervened. I met and married an admirable man. I sold my condo and moved to Ontario with him. Initially, we lived in the house he already owned. It badly needed updating, but there were enough rooms that I could have an office with one wall of bookshelves. I had flashbacks because the cold and damp basement reminded me of the cellar at The Hovel and it had the same red-and-black low-pile carpet I moved away from many years before!

Eventually, we purchased a townhouse-style condo. A lower-level walkout and large windows in my office overlooked an expanse of lawn that attracted deer and wild turkeys. I refused to put drapes over the windows, which caused a few heated discussions between us. The main floor included a skylight that bathed the room with brightness even on moonlit nights. But shared accommodation requires negotiation and we debated which of our personal items we could display. In the end, his mounted fish and sports memorabilia circled the walls in the lower level and we carefully combined our separate pieces of art into a joint gallery in the upper level. My books got shelved and my quilts were draped around the house, but my Reddi-wip dolls stayed in their shoe box on a shelf.

Two weeks after we celebrated our twenty-third anniversary, my husband died from leukemia. I rattled around in the huge space surrounded by remnants of his amazing life. My family and many friends were still in Manitoba and I decided to move home. During several trips to Winnipeg, a real estate agent toured me around the city that had expanded outward during the decades I lived "down east." As we entered a newly conceived subdivision, I asked aloud, "Where the hell are we?" I didn't recognize the city where I had pumped gas as a teenager.

In the end, I chose an apartment-style condo because I will have no yard work. The snow is shovelled and the lawn is mowed by invisible workers paid to do the job. My neighbours and I share the responsibility of paying for roof repairs, if needed, and other areas of the building that require improving.

There is no basement! My real estate agent showed me a multi-level unit that had a lower-level walk-out, but

I still felt the weight of the structure above me and the space was shadowy in the farthest corners.

Three bedrooms allow me to have guests and space to create. My office alcove is hidden from view and my perpetual mess of research, a reference library, and office supplies goes unseen by visitors. The closets accommodate clothing, but also have shelves containing boxes that are easily reached and labelled with their contents. All my books are on shelves and my Reddi-wip dolls that Mum contrived to get for me have pride of place in a niche beside my bedroom.

I have left the wall of windows in my living room uncovered. I feel safe and secure watching Prairie storms build and then burst with lightning and torrents of rain. In winter, as snow falls beyond the glass, I wrap up in an afghan Mum made and read a book by lamplight.

I reflect on the houses of my childhood and how they influenced my attitude towards living spaces. As I stand looking east through my large windows on a darkening winter afternoon, the St. Boniface Cathedral rises above the trees and the pointed roof of the Royal Canadian Mint in the distance looks like the fin of a shark. I know what caused me to fall in love with this space the moment I walked through the door: this light-filled condo is everything I loved about Wildwood and nothing I hated about The Hovel.

The three houses that sheltered me in childhood are gone, either razed or bulldozed or collapsed. The farmhouse was the first to go. It was burned by the farm's new owner along with the barn, granaries, and chicken coop. An excavator flattened The Hovel. A developer purchased it and the house next door—the one with the picket fence that I climbed over—combining the two properties. He built a four-plex, tearing out the apple tree to make room for a garage. The Haunted Acres still stands with unknown owners, but it played such a small role in my life that I discount it. Sadly, Wildwood simply fell in upon itself after my cousin moved out, leaving it neglected for many years. His son inherited the property and built a new home rather than live in a house crafted by people he never knew.

If I have a regret about this space, it is that Mum did not live to visit me here, share some tea, and play a game of Scrabble. I believe I have her to thank for this condo because she encouraged me to get my degree, was proud of my first newspaper job and thrilled when I got better jobs and promotions, and couldn't hide her joy when she visited me in my first home with its dearth of furniture. I feel her spirit now and know she would be happy that I moved beyond her reality. I absorbed her dreams and turned them into a life that I hope honours her struggles. In the end, Mum's greatest achievement was giving us the tools to help us live productive lives. She never stopped looking out the windows of our houses to see a better place in the world for all of us.

ACKNOWLEDGEMENTS

MY SIBLINGS, Lynette and Edward, have always supported me in every endeavour I have undertaken. Their memories of the farmhouse were invaluable and without them reminding me I may have gotten many details incorrect. Sadly, Edward, who read to me as I lay in my crib smiling at him, did not live to see me get this book published.

Thank you to the descendants of Iva and Harley Bradley for allowing me to use them as supporting players in a very personal story about family resilience.

A number of good friends sustained me while I agonized over which details needed to be included in a story about an ordinary family who struggled through some daunting life challenges. Thank you to Alex Merrill, who read one of the earliest versions of the book and helped me understand the memoir-writing process better. Susan McLennan, Val Mace, Andrea Geary, Colleen Edmunds, and Cindy Spear Ross read bits and pieces of the manuscript, proofread Draft #9, or commiserated through the submission process, helping me develop marketing plans and commenting on my latest attempt at a catchy synopsis. All encouraged me to keep going. I wish I had space to acknowledge all the friends who celebrated with me when Heritage House expressed interest in *Naomi's Houses*.

My first editor, Ellie Barton, helped me massage the manuscript into a structure that would make sense to readers. Even when the cutting and pasting and rearranging didn't work, she urged me to keep looking for another solution to solve structural issues.

Finally, the team at Heritage House, especially editor Kate Kennedy, kept me on track and made many valuable suggestions to get *Naomi's Houses* into print. When, at age four, I told my mother that I was going to write a book someday, she didn't laugh. But she would never have believed that decades later Heritage House would agree with me that her story deserves to be in print.

ABOUT THE AUTHOR

AWARD-WINNING agricultural journalist Rosalie I. Tennison has never forgotten her rural roots. Her long career has taken her from rural weekly newspapers to a small-town radio station to agricultural trade magazines to the communications department of the Faculty of Agriculture and Food Sciences at the University of Manitoba. She is the recipient of a gold citation from the Canadian Farm Writers' Federation and is a gold-medal winner of a 2022 Canadian Online Publishing Award. While she loves meeting producers in the fields where they work, she enjoys returning to the warmth of her Winnipeg condo to curl up with her cat and a good book.